WHEN THE

When the Mind is Blind

William Doyle

DOYLE'S PUBLICATIONS

First published 2002

Published in the UK by Doyle's Publications
P.O. Box 79, Hove, BN3 4WH.

ISBN 0 9542801 0 5

Book design and production for the publisher by
Bookprint Creative Services,
P.O. Box 827, BN21 3YJ, England.
Printed in Great Britain.

ACKNOWLEDGEMENTS

This book is dedicated to the many families who struggle with the difficulties dementia imposes upon them.

My story could not have been told without the help of one family in particular. Indeed I am grateful for the love, tolerance and forgiveness of many caring people. I shall remember their kindness with affection and lasting gratitude.

I give glory to God for my ministry, and bless the names of those whose lives have touched my own.

PREFACE

I have waited until now to write this story. All I have written is true and the people are real, but most of the names and places are false. It was my privilege to know the characters personally, and I have their permission to relate these experiences as they happened.

I have witnessed their courage, faith, friendliness, and acts of love, kindness and compassion, and I believe the story should now be told. Its purpose, is two-fold. Firstly, I want to provide some insight and encouragement to families with relatives suffering from the loss of social skills, personal awareness and memory impairment arising from the illness known as *dementia*. This is a condition which is characterised by behavioural changes, including memory disturbance, deterioration of the intellect, emotional problems and changes in the personality, accompanied by confusion and language difficulties.

Secondly I want to tell of a "love affair" which blossomed as the writer encountered it in his relationship with these wonderful people.

I have not attempted to address all the clinical details of this illness, which slowly dismantles the human personality. To do so would take us down the "text book" path, and this is not my intention. I wish to stay as close as possible to the people involved, and to relate their coping strategies.

In a world estranged from God, even sceptical about His presence in human affairs, some of the things I relate may sound unbelievable. Please keep an open mind and, when you have finished reading the book, judge for yourself.

My story proves the reality of the living God and the way in which His Spirit shines on those who love Him and seek His company. It takes the reader down the "ancient path", revealing God's abiding presence and unfailing care.

As I followed the lives of the principal characters of this book, I came to realise that they experienced, by God's grace, what I can only describe as a new dimension to life, bringing inspiration to the spirit and peace to the weary soul. And I discovered that this is something available to us all; it is not confined to just a few select people. When we keep the windows of the soul open in the knowledge that God loves us, His love will flow through us to others.

May His presence touch the lives of each one of you, and grace you with His peace and joy as you journey through this life to the kingdom our Father has prepared for you.

William Doyle

"Infirmus eram, et visitastis me"
"I was sick . . . and you visited me"
Matthew 25:36

KATHLEEN

ONE

The village of Cowley Down lay to the south of Highton Hills. If there is such a place as the highest heaven then its beauty and peace is surely reflected here in the serenity of this countryside. In this picturesque village, Kathleen lived with her parents, Gordon and Mary Whittacker.

Kathleen had been married for just two short years when one foggy night her husband had failed to return home from his work. He had been fatally injured in a car accident and died of his injuries a few hours later. Kathleen was heartbroken, and after a brief interval had leased out her two-bedroom apartment, and was now living with her parents.

Gordon and Mary had lived together happily for many years; indeed this coming weekend they were to celebrate their Ruby Wedding and Kathleen was making the final preparations. Her parents had worked hard all their lives; they deserved this special day, because they were both special people.

Gordon had been a considerate husband and a kind

father. He always understood Kathleen's growing pains and she had relied on his wise counsel, his love and sense of humour to soothe her anxieties in her teenage years. He was a tower of strength when she lost her husband.

Gordon was now aged 68 and showing signs of poor health. Several years before he had been made redundant from his work as an electronic engineer, but had kept himself occupied with his garden and the small business he had set up. His wife Mary noticed his failing health with growing concern, but he always insisted that there was nothing wrong. As time past, however, he neglected paperwork and was becoming more and more forgetful and sometimes aggressive.

Today, both he and Mary had been out visiting one of Kathleen's colleagues, Aston Wills, and other members of the psychiatric team at Coopersfield Hospital in Barchester, seven miles away. Kathleen was eagerly awaiting their return. When she heard her parents walking up the garden path, she opened the door to let them in and quickly but quietly settled them both in the living room.

Tea was soon prepared. Kathleen saw the rigid and absent gaze on her father's face and knew that everything she had heard about Alzheimer's disease was now facing them with its awful consequences. She put her arm around her mother who had remained silent, but who was thinking of the illness known as the "silent enemy" that slowly dismantles the human personality and leaves in its wake a shattered immune system.

It was an illness still shrouded in a certain amount of mystery, and Kathleen, knowing of the disturbed behaviour which accompanies dementia, prayed silently that it would be minimal. She also thought of what her mother would have to face as the condition became progressively worse, and Gordon's memory failed.

Her father had always encouraged Kathleen to have high hopes and aspirations, but now doubts about the future were entering her mind. Suddenly Gordon sat upright and said, "Oh, Kathleen, I didn't know you had come to visit. Let me get you a drink. I know what you like." The remainder of the afternoon was spent quietly talking with her mother about the future.

Kathleen remembered that she had some lecture notes on the subject of dementia, given to her by a minister. The Revd Brian Brookes had worked in the field of Community Psychiatric Medicine and had a special interest in illnesses affecting the elderly. After searching through several boxes and cupboards later on that day, Kathleen eventually unearthed the notes.

She settled down to read her lecture notes, which she had headed, "The Quiet Epidemic."

Many names have been given to the symptoms of memory loss and the impairment of the reasoning capacity in adults. Some of the most common include senility, pre-senile dementia, Alzheimer's disease, hardening of the arteries and organic brain syndrome.

Dementia is not a mental illness, but a symptom of an underlying disorder; the word *dementia* is used in a specific way; it means the loss or impairment of a person's mental abilities. Dementia describes a group of symptoms which arise from a number of diseases including infections such as meningitis, encephalitis, Creutzfeldt-Jakob and HIV.

Toxins also have to be considered, as do metabolic disorders and degenerative diseases such as Huntington's, Parkinson's, Pick's and Alzheimer's. None of these may be responsible; nor should we assume that dementia is inevitable because of these diseases – there may be other reasons not yet known.

Kathleen glanced across at her father sitting silently in his chair. Looking at him resting so peacefully, it was hard to imagine the impending deterioration that would play havoc with his mind and cause him to be blind to the realities of life; but the truth was evident when he was awake. She wondered if he knew that as the illness progressed it was likely that he would become incontinent, confused and incoherent with mindless wandering.

Going back to her notes she recalled Brian saying that Alzheimer's disease appears to be the most common cause of irreversible dementia in adults, but there is much that can be done to make the patient comfortable, and to give the carer a sense of control over the situation. Kathleen wanted this for her mother, since Mary suffered from partial deafness and would need all the help she could get.

Brian's lectures were always held in the annexe of the post-graduate library of Coopersfield Hospital in Barchester. They had proved to be popular and several nurses had given up their free time to attend. One of them, Rebecca, was a post-graduate nurse whose grandmother had dementia of the multi-infarct type (a series of strokes within the brain). She had asked Brian to explain it to her.

"Multi-infarct dementia progresses in a step-like manner," explained Brian. "The patient may not seem to get worse for a time, indeed may even appear a little better. The course of the illness varies with the specific disorder and the individual."

Observing the concern on Rebecca's face, Brian went on to explain that it was considered to be the second most common cause of dementia; and that the repeated strokes in the brain often destroyed cells affecting memory, speech and co-ordination, causing impairment or even breakdown in the transmitter system. The chances were that her grandmother would be spared the knowledge and the distress about what was happening, though she might have occasional insights which were not lasting and which would eventually be forgotten altogether.

Kathleen was sitting on the sofa absorbed in her notes while Mary sat close to her husband. Caring for a person with dementia was not going to be easy, but Kathleen knew that many families and their confused relatives still manage to experience joy and happiness. After all, her father was still a unique human being who could be loved even when in a deeply troubled state.

As Kathleen continued to persue the notes she had taken from Brian's lectures she was reminded of Martin, a medical student in his final year.

Martin was considered the most thoughtful man in his class. He knew the blessedness of silently lifting up his soul to God when he was in the most pressing of circumstances and the busiest of ward routines. He was known to say, "Nothing can make up for direct communion with God. Even working in His service can sometimes be exhausting; one has to be renewed from above."

Martin was present at one of Brian's lectures and he had asked, "I have heard that memory has positive and negative aspects, would the speaker comment on this?"

"The fact that memory is fragmentary should not alarm us," Brian answered. "Indeed, it is God's gift to us that we do not remember every detail of all our experiences. How else could we put behind us the dark clouds of the past, some of which may be too painful to experience yet again?

"We also have to take into consideration that memory loss may be voluntary on the part of some elderly persons. This often happens when they lose family or friends. Faced with the sad knowledge that they are alone, they attempt to protect themselves from reality. Memory only returns when they feel loved and needed again. Benign forgetfulness is not a mark of senility and we should guard against the assumption that because a person is old and forgetful that they are senile.

"Burying painful memories and remembering pleasant ones is characteristic of young and old. Life is meaningful as long as we have reasonably good health and someone who cares."

Brian paused for a moment then said, "I don't personally advocate the method used in some counselling techniques of taking the counsellee back to the past. The past is finished. Why put a person through pain and torment again, or remind them of their mistakes and foolishness? There's a passage in the Bible which says 'I will remember their sin no more.'"

Brian would often refer to God's Word to illustrate a point, and Kathleen recalled the smile on Brian's face as he had added, "If Omniscience is prepared to forget, should we be alarmed that we cannot remember everything?

"One of the miracles of divine grace is positive forgetfulness," he went on. "If we could recall everything we might easily become overwhelmed, so forgetfulness has a positive side to it. There are bright and dark days in everyone's life; we retain most of our memories, but not all are recalled."

Martin had found comfort from those words, and that was what Kathleen needed at this trying time. If only she could speak to Brian, but he had moved away to other tasks for his Lord.

Kathleen was beginning to realise she was going to have to stay strong and maintain her faith in God no matter what happened. Her father's wise counsel had in the past helped to sustain her faith. And she remembered the strength of Brian's faith. He was fond of saying that "faith has great cosmic significance."

She once heard him tell his students, "Faith sees the invisible, hears the inaudible, touches the intangible, believes the One who's indivisible. Faith is deaf to doubts, dumb to discouragement, blind to impossibilities, and impervious to failure."

Brian had never married, but those who knew him sensed that he had once known the love of a woman. He never talked about it, but he would often say, "There are many unloving situations in the world today, but love has a way of changing things. Without it we are easily deceived about where happiness lies."

Kathleen had often thought he would have made a fine husband and father. He was kind and considerate, generous and playful. But she noticed he was unmoved by the flashing eyes of his female students.

She often wondered if he was lonely, and if so, how he coped with it. Whenever she saw him he always seemed to be surrounded by many people.

Didn't the Lord God say somewhere that it was "not good for man to be alone"? It is by interacting with others that we gain our identity and learn who we are. Brian always seemed confident and self-assured. Perhaps his self-reliance came from relying on God – to him a firm reality.

While loneliness is at the heart of human existence, some people are well able to manage. These were the thoughts going through Kathleen's mind as she reflected on her memories of this quietly-spoken, unassuming man. She felt herself drawn to him, and imagined his strong arms around her and his face close to hers.

Then, almost in a whisper, Kathleen quoted some

words from a Spanish proverb: "Where there is no love, pour love in and you will draw love out."

From his chair her father said, "St John of the Cross."

"What did you say?" asked Kathleen.

"You were quoting words from St John of the Cross," he replied.

Kathleen slept peacefully that night knowing her father's long-term memory was intact – for the time being.

TWO

Mary knew nothing of dementia and even less about how to deal with Gordon's strange behaviour arising from it. There were days when he was co-operative, but the very next day he would be impossible.

Dressing him became a struggle; if Mary left him to dress himself she would find two socks on one foot, his under-vest on top of his shirt, buttons in wrong holes, and his shoe laces left undone. She overcame these problems by using Velcro and slip-on shoes.

As Gordon's illness progressed communicating with him became increasingly difficult, and his eating habits deteriorated. Sometimes he would not use a knife and fork, but lift the plate to his mouth – or not eat at all. Mary soon learned to keep mealtimes simple, with little change in routine. Several foods on the plate meant Gordon had to make a choice which, Mary came to realise, he could not do.

Incontinence was also a problem. Gordon could never reach the toilet in time, and when he was very confused he would "go" in the cupboard, or behind the television.

Mary gradually learnt to deal with Gordon's odd behaviour, and not to get upset about it, but some days were more difficult than others.

Sometimes Mary would recall that it hadn't always been like this. Memories of their time together would come flooding into her mind. She would go over and take him by the hand. He would smile and she would remember how handsome he had been, how energetic.

She remembered their brief honeymoon on the sandy shores of Living Water Bay.

The sea was rough on their first day, yet he had insisted they walk along the beach. The wind blew salty spray against them and she remembered the way his hair blew carelessly in the wind, and his tall, slim, strong physique cut fine lines against the clear blue sky. His illness couldn't erase that memory of him; she would treasure it as long as she lived.

They sat together in silence as Mary continued to recall that first day. The wind had died down and Gordon had run on ahead and found two large rocks, which formed a perfect seat for them both. The sea was growing calmer; white-capped waves moved in measured cadence across the surface of the sea and mysteriously disappeared as they neared the shore.

It was all a long time ago. Looking deeply into Gordon's eyes Mary whispered, "Can you remember your love letters to me, when we were young? Now we're old and past our youth, but you're like the rays of the setting sun. Each beam goes on mile after mile and reflects the sunshine of your smile. I remember every letter, each touch and soft caress. You brought to my life such passion and charm."

He is still handsome, she thought, but this illness had aged him. Being old is not so bad as long as we keep away from mirrors, Mary thought to herself.

As the weeks went by Kathleen encouraged her mother to allow Gordon to attend a day centre. "He'll enjoy it and you'll have a well-earned rest," she insisted.

Mary was reluctant to let her husband go, but lately she had been having pains in her chest and she felt tired. So she agreed.

"Good. I'll see to it," Kathleen reassured her. She immediately called her colleague Aston Wills on the phone.

Mary was quite impressed with the standard of care Gordon received during his visits to the Day Centre. There was a family atmosphere and several hours of structured therapeutic programmes, including music, entertainment and hairdressing. She observed that Gordon was a little more manageable at home, and he looked forward to his "outings" as he called them. And Mary was feeling the benefit of having time for herself. She continued to enjoy several months of respite care.

One morning Mary was seated in her favourite armchair listening to Mozart, with the sun streaming through the windows of Primrose Cottage, which had been their home for 35 years. There was a knock at the door. Mary answered it and smiled on seeing a huge bunch of flowers in the arms of Kelly, her next door neighbour. "These came earlier when you were out taking Gordon to the Centre," said Kelly.

Mary read the card attached to the flowers. It was signed "Your friend, Brian." Kathleen had often spoken of Brian with more than admiration, Mary thought. Placing the flowers in a vase of fresh water she continued listening to Mozart.

Gordon was due home at five o'clock, but at 4.30 the telephone rang. It was the nurse in charge of the Day Centre. "Mrs Whittacker, we've just admitted your husband to hospital. We're very sorry to give you this news over the phone, but he was violent and confused. He attacked one of the other patients this afternoon, then collapsed. He was taken to the psychiatric unit at Coopersfield, Ward 12."

Mary's heart sank and she was crying as she ordered a taxi to take her to the hospital. Ward 12 was on the third floor and along a corridor which seemed a mile long. She arrived to find Gordon looking rested.

"We had to admit him," the sister said quietly. "He's

sedated, so just sit with him or come back whenever you wish."

Mary sat for about an hour, Gordon never spoke or opened his eyes. She thought of the times she was angry – not with Gordon, but with what was happening to him. She was especially angry when he wandered off and she had to search for him. Often she would find him in a neighbour's garden picking their flowers, or in the next street talking to a cat.

She was always afraid he might wander too far or get hurt, and her fear made her angry, but afterwards she was always sorry. Mary had confided her thoughts to Aston Wills during one of his visits. "Does God really care?" she asked him.

"It's understandable if you get angry at the situation you are in, angry that this has happened to you, angry that you are trapped in this network of twenty-four hour care. Even people with a strong religious faith question how God can do such a thing. You should not feel guilty about your anger with God. We all have to struggle with this question."

Mary's heart sank as she sat watching her husband lying there so helpless. He was a shadow of the man he used to be, she thought. A nurse came over every so often to check on Gordon's condition. Mary knew that Gordon's behaviour had been the result of the illness and nothing personal. He had lost the ability to take charge of himself and to make decisions.

Mary wiped the tears from her eyes and had just decided to leave, when a woman in her mid-fifties, with glasses on the end of her nose, came over and spoke to her in a soft, west country accent. "Excuse me," she said. "I couldn't help noticing that you've sat there for almost an hour. Can I get you a cup of tea?"

Mary began to cry again.

"I'm off duty in a few moments," the woman said. "Why don't we both go to the cafeteria and we can talk." Mary looked closely at the mild mannered woman dressed in a green smock-like dress. She had a sweet smile, her hair was tied neatly and she had a friendly manner. "All right," Mary answered.

During the next thirty minutes Mary learned that Isabel was one of the voluntary helpers on Ward 12. She had a special interest in helping elderly mentally infirm people, providing companionship, sympathy and a listening ear.

"That sounds like a difficult job," Mary said, after listening to Isabel speak so enthusiastically about her work.

"I like it," Isabel answered. "I was an Occupational Therapist when I was younger."

They talked a few minutes longer and then Isabel

said, "I must be going. It was nice meeting you; perhaps we'll meet again." She turned to go, then looking back at Mary said, "I have a book which might interest you. You may borrow it if you wish. It's called *The Unconscious Interlude,* written by a clergyman. I hope that won't put you off." She smiled and added, "But I'd like it back."

Mary returned to Ward 12 to kiss Gordon goodnight, and then she caught a taxi home. Kathleen had arrived home late having been away for most of the day on a visit to another hospital.

Mary assured her daughter there was no need to pay Gordon a visit at this late hour. Nothing more could be done for the time being. The ward sister had said they wanted to keep Gordon in for a few days, and would telephone if there was any change.

Kathleen pointed to the flowers on the corner table. "Are these from someone special?" she asked.

"Oh, I almost forgot!" said Mary. "Those came for you. Yes, you could say from someone special," she added, hiding a smile and watching her daughter out of the corner of her eye. Did she secretly love this Brian of hers? If she did, she didn't reveal her feelings. Mary pushed the idea out of her mind, after all love has many languages.

"Kathy, there's a meeting of the Carers Association on

Thursday afternoon. I'd like to go, are you free to take me?"

"Of course. Who's the speaker?"

"Someone with a special interest in illnesses affecting the elderly," Mary responded, closing her eyes.

"It's time we were in bed, mother. I'm whacked. We'll go and see dad in the morning. Goodnight."

THREE

Kathleen never had any regrets about resuming her nursing career. Coopersfield Hospital had a good reputation and once she was established her management skills were recognised and she was put in charge of the EMI department, which cared for patients suffering from physical and mental disorders affecting the elderly.

Arriving for duty the following morning Kathleen learnt that her father was to remain in hospital because of a suspected infection, which may have formed on his lungs.

When Mary arrived at the hospital, Gordon was half-asleep and a nurse was making him comfortable.

"There's a parcel here for you," said the nurse, pointing to a brown envelope on the side table.

"Thank you," Mary responded absently stooping to kiss Gordon and whispering in his ear how much she loved him. She opened the envelope and found the book, which Isabel had promised to lend her.

Putting the book aside Mary sat watching Gordon, thinking how frail and helpless he looked. She thought of his loving ways, his sharp mind, his generous nature and love of children and things of nature. How the "silent enemy" had changed all that!

Suddenly Mary was aware of a young man standing quietly at the foot of the bed. "Oh, I didn't see you there," she murmured.

"I didn't mean to startle you," the young man said, "but I'd like to say hello. My name's Brian. I used to be a chaplain here."

He was dressed casually, stood about six feet tall, and had thick brown wavy hair. Mary liked the look of him and smiled. His eyes smiled back and Mary thought he seemed like someone with a real concern for those who were hurting.

He turned to look at Gordon. "I'm very sorry to see your husband like this. If there is anything I can do . . ."
Mary remained silent for a while and then asked, "How do you know he is my husband?"

"Please forgive me. I should have introduced myself properly," Brian replied. "Your daughter Kathy and I were on the same team when I was chaplain here."

Mary nodded knowingly. So this was the man who had stirred Kathleen's heart!

"Padre, will you come quickly," said a nurse at that moment, and Brian was gone.

*

The carer's meeting was held in the hospital library annexe. Kathleen led her mother to a seat close to the front of the room. There were just a few minutes before the meeting was due to start.

"So who's the speaker then?" Kathleen whispered.

"You'll see," her mother smiled. At that moment Brian walked on, took his place and began to speak.

"You represent the 1.25 million carers in Britain. A large proportion of them are family members and are themselves in poor health. Some may be young mothers having to raise children and care for ailing relatives at the same time. Others may have responsible jobs, so it's important that you have some time to yourselves."

Mary glanced at Kathleen. Her eyes were fixed on Brian as he outlined the merits of "respite care" programmes and family support groups up and down the country. He spoke about the values of music therapy, orientation exercises and other psychological treatments offered by professional staff in hospitals and day centres. All of these could make life easier for the carer.

"So many people try to cope by themselves, but it's so much easier when you share the problems of caring for a relative with dementia", he assured his listeners.

Brian spoke for an hour and time was allowed for questions. He answered them all to everyone's satisfaction. The last question came from a young mother of two children.

"I get so worried when I have to leave my mother. Often she doesn't know what day it is, or where she lives. She turns on the gas fire but doesn't light it. She can't find the toilet or even dress properly. I sometimes wonder what life is all about."

Brian looked at the woman with compassion, seeing the distress on her face. She wanted some answers.

"We each have our own ideas about the meaning of life," he replied. "Some people find strength from religious beliefs. Others may hold none at all and yet have a strong sense of self-worth. From my own experience I think it wise to face life as it is, not as we feel it ought to be. Unexpected events intrude into our lives and we have to deal with them without being too hard on ourselves or others. Life has its complications, but we can overcome them more easily when we know the love of a friend and have a commitment to God, who created us."

There was silence in the room as Brian spoke. "Problems in life can only be resolved by means of a right relationship with God," he continued. "The further we move away from God, the less we experience joy or peace in the soul. And some things cannot be put right. We can only try to make amends – we can't go back.

"Many people say they are tired of life; but the truth is

that no one was ever tired of life – they are tired of being half dead while they are alive! What is needed is a transformation by the indwelling of God's Holy Spirit. Then they become spiritually alive, filled with the life Jesus came to give."

Mary was thrilled to hear this message of hope. It was just what she needed to bolster her flagging spirit. As she listened to the confident, reassuring voice, it began to dawn on her how little she understood the significance of joy in the Christian life. She had often regarded it as something secondary, and not as proof that God does indeed satisfy us.

Mary sensed the love and knowledge behind Brian's words which gave out such warmth and affection.

Brian paused a moment, and then lowering his voice he said, "Questions about life are not answered by doing or not doing this or that, but by these words: 'Come unto me all ye that labour and are heavy laden, and I will give you rest.' The weakest person, the worst sinner, can draw on the resurrection life of Christ, and He will fill the soul with faith and determination, and help us through our difficulties."

As Brian walked away from the podium there was thunderous applause, which Kathleen knew would make him feel uncomfortable. He was fond of saying, "We should give God the glory."

There were many people waiting to speak with him afterwards, so Mary and Kathleen browsed among the books. "I have all of Brian's books except one," she told her mother. "I wonder if it's here?"

"What's it called?" Mary asked.

"The Unconscious Interlude," Kathleen replied.

"Don't worry, I have it."

"You?"

"Yes, a friend lent it to me," Mary murmured.

At that moment the figure of Brian Brookes towered over them. "Well, this is a surprise," he smiled. "Hello, Mary."

"You know my mother?" said Kathleen, surprised.

"O yes, we're old friends,' he replied, grinning widely.

"Why don't you come and have supper with us on Saturday evening? We can talk more easily," Mary said. Kathleen could hardly believe her ears; she had wanted to ask him home so many times before. She waited for his reply.

"I'd like nothing better. Will 7 o'clock suit you?"

"That will be fine," Mary beamed. "We'd better be going, Kathleen." She was in one of her assertive moods and Kathleen knew better than to protest. She smiled at Brian. "We look forward to seeing you on Saturday evening."

The following afternoon Kathleen was walking

towards the boardroom in Coopersfield Hospital. She had been accused of racism by one of the agency nurses on her ward and summoned to appear before a tribunal. As she was passing the chapel she looked at her watch. "I've just got time," she said to herself, and went inside.

She had not been seated long before the door opened and in walked Brian.

"Kathy! What a lovely surprise," he said in his gentle tones.

"What are *you* doing here?" Kathleen blurted out.

"Is something troubling you?" he asked.

"Why are you here?" She insisted.

"I'm helping out during my study leave," he replied, in an attempt to calm her. "You're on duty?" he said, looking at her uniform. Kathleen told him what had happened, and how in a few minutes she was to appear before the hospital complaints committee to answer the allegations.

"You – a racist?" he laughed. "Don't worry about it, God will vindicate you."

"That's all right for you to say," She exploded.

"I mean it," he continued. "What time is your appointment?"

"In ten minutes," Kathleen murmured.

"Good. Then we just have time for a prayer," Brian said, with a twinkle in his eye. Kathleen had seen that look before. She knew that he believed no day is well spent without communication with God.

Brian sat down next to Kathleen, closed his eyes and said, "Father in heaven, we send thoughts of love to those we shall meet today. Instil in them and us clear and inspired minds. Help us to realise that if we consecrate our lives to love, we shall discover that we have the strength to meet difficult situations with courage. If we consecrate our lives to wisdom, we'll find knowledge and inspiration to see things clearly. If we consecrate our lives to truth, we'll follow your ways and believe in your Word.

"Now, you must be going," he said. Kathleen left without saying a word and walked the short distance to the boardroom.

She had a few minutes to spare and sat waiting in a chair opposite the entrance to the boardroom. It wasn't long before the door opened and out walked a tall, distinguished man with thick, greying hair, wearing a clerical collar. Behind him came the unit manager accompanied by the Chairman of the hospital Management Committee and two other doctors.

One was Bashir Vishnu, who was on a visit to England and had taken time to look up his old friend, the Rev James Brookes. The other was Indi Ramanhansa.

Dr Vishnu was a specialist in paediatrics and highly

regarded by the World Health Organisation. He had been invited to attend a special meeting of the Royal Society for the Promotion of Health by Dr Ramanhansa, a consultant at one of the London hospitals where Kathleen had worked as senior sister in the operating theatre several years before.

When Dr Ramanhansa saw Kathleen he stared for a moment and then walked over to where she was seated.

"Aren't you Kathleen Whittacker?" he said, smiling.

"I am," she replied, getting to her feet. Kathleen's working relationship with Dr R, as he was known, had been close and very successful. He was sorry when she left to get married. They embraced each other and spoke for several minutes.

The small party which had emerged from the board-room observed the friendly scene. Kathleen was not called to answer the allegations and the case was dismissed!

As Kathleen returned to her duties and walked passed the chapel she smiled a big "thank you."

When Kathleen arrived home that evening her mother asked, "Well, how did you get on?"

Kathleen told her.

"I'm so relieved," Mary sighed. "But who was the tall distinguished clergyman you mentioned?"

"I'm not sure. I think he's the new hospital chaplain

who has care of St Andrew's during the interregnum. But there was something about his eyes," Kathleen murmured quietly to herself.

Mary knew Brian only through Kathleen's reports, the brief bedside meeting, and her recent conversation, so she was looking forward to his visit. His personality and his message seem so completely bound up with one another that when she opened the door to him she knew there and then that she was going to like him.

"Do come in; I'm pleased you could come," she smiled. Kathleen joined them a few moments later. Brian rose from his chair as Kathleen entered the living room. She was wearing a black dress, her hair lay loose on her shoulders. Round her neck she wore her grandmother's pearls.

Brian spoke first: "Hello, Kathleen." She held out her hand and he clasped it firmly. Her heart was racing, but she controlled her feelings and said, "I'm delighted you have come to visit us." They exchanged smiles and Mary offered them both a drink.

"It's a joy to have you here, Brian," said Mary. Then she told him about the events leading up to Gordon's admission to hospital. He listened carefully to all she had to say and then said "Life is very cruel sometimes, isn't it? But you will find strength to deal with it. I know just how you feel."

Mary realised this was why he was so well liked and so qualified to be a pastor. There were no religious platitudes, no endless hushed sympathy. Here was someone saying, yes, life can be brutal, and it was all right to be angry and to grieve.

During supper the conversation took many turns. Mary learned that Brian valued the sacraments of the church, but was concerned about the lack of understanding in society about the spiritual meaning behind them.

It was obvious he valued the spiritual life, but acknowledged the difficulties and the struggles. "My mentor used to say, 'saints are ordinary people who just keep going'," he said laughingly, "so I suppose we must keep going."

After the meal Brian offered to help with the dishes. When they were settled in the living room drinking coffee, Mary asked, "How does the person with dementia grieve?" In her mind was the thought of what might happen to Gordon if she were to die first.

Kathleen, surprised at her mother's question, looked at Brian and waited. It was some time before he spoke. He sensed the reason for her question and said quietly, "The answer to this question is not fully known. It would appear that dementia sufferers go through the same process of bereavement as anyone else. There is a darkness of uncertainty we all have to face sometime."

He went on, "There's a word in Isaiah, which should help when we're faced with difficult questions. The writer says, 'Let him trust in the name of the Lord, and rely on his God.'

"I think we need to do this more often, Mary, and not feel that God has suspended His blessing, or even that going to church has become difficult, which in some cases may be true. I would encourage you to keep on walking in faith, no matter how dismal things appear."

He was quiet for a moment, then said, "A bereaved person is often disturbed or agitated, indeed, they may lose interest in their personal appearance. But all this disappears with reassurance, stimulation, the development of new relationships and the passage of time.

"It's not so for those suffering from dementia, however, because the person is not able to form ideas and has no consistent knowledge of what is happening.

"My personal view is that sufferers from dementia are familiar with grief in the early stages of the illness though they may not be able to express it coherently. Later, global ideas are not so easily formed and recall is minimal; so in a sense they are spared the grief which healthy people face and are able to deal with eventually.

"Mary, many people are held in bondage by invisible

chains. They are bound by fear, poor habits and oppression which torments them. Dismiss those thoughts about what might happen if you should die before your husband."

Mary looked surprised that Brian had read her thoughts.

"Whose kingdom is it, anyway?" he said, with a smile. "When the time comes for either of you finally to fall asleep, your most joyful moment will be when you surrender to the Lord; he will take all the pain away, and death will lose its sting.

"Now, I think that's quite enough of that subject," he said, laughingly. "If you don't mind I'd like some more coffee, please." Kathleen and Brian exchanged glances as Mary filled the cups.

It was getting late and Brian had an early start the next morning. He thanked Mary for her hospitality and prepared to leave. "You must come again," she said.

"I would like that. But may I bring someone with me? He's a very special friend, who would appreciate your cooking."

"Of course," Mary agreed, wondering who this mysterious friend might be.

"I'll see you to the door," said Kathleen. As she opened it for him to pass through, she said, "your visit meant a lot to my mother."

Suddenly she wanted desperately to be held in his arms, to feel his lips on hers, but held herself in check knowing that it would be so easy to be swept along by sexual desires. She didn't share society's view that without an active sex life we are inadequate human beings. No, she would wait. Promiscuity was not an option, faithfulness and commitment must be the key elements in any relationship.

After all, true love is not a feeling by which we are overwhelmed, she reassured herself, even though deep inside her there was still a yearning to be swept off her feet.

Brian made no attempt to move towards her, yet Kathleen was reassured by the memory of hearing him teach his students that it is a basic necessity of life to love and be loved. "We do not choose to fall in love," he once said.

Giving her a big smile, Brian thanked her and walked off into the night.

FOUR

On Sunday, Mary decided to go to church and visit Gordon in the afternoon. The pew inside the eleventh-century parish church was already beginning to feel uncomfortable as she waited for the service to begin. St Andrew's church was typical of the Norman churches built at that time.

This was the church in which she and Gordon had been married. Mary had vivid memories of their wedding day, and smiled as she recalled that the most important thing in the church as far as Gordon was concerned had been the nave roof, with its oak tie beams, constructed without king posts or brackets, and resting only on wall plates positioned on top of the outside walls.

As Mary mused, the choir and clergy made their entrance. The angelic sound of the choristers as they lifted their voices to the strains of the Bevington organ, echoed round the solid walls of this house of prayer as they filed past.

After the lessons were read, the preacher, the Rev Canon James Brookes, took his place in the pulpit. His ministry had been a varied one. He had been a parish priest, a school chaplain, principal of a school in Delhi for a number of years, and then vice-principal of Barchester Theological College. He was now retired, and helping out during the interregnum in Cowley Down parish church.

As he stood there in the pulpit Mary couldn't help but notice a striking resemblance in style to Brian. Impossible, she thought. She couldn't hear clearly all that was being said, but caught the words, "A saint is someone who is righteous in God's sight; but what makes a saint? Saints are in this world but not of it; cheerful when things are difficult; they push on when they want to stand still, and keep silent when it's the wrong time to talk, that's all!"

Mary remembered Brian saying something similar, but shrugged off the thought. She paid special attention when the Canon started talking about health matters. "When we are ill, we don't want to be reminded of our lack of tolerance, our unbelief or pride; no, we need more than anything to be reminded that we are loved. We need sympathy. Not cold moralising, but warm compassion."

The service ended with the hymn, 'King of Glory, King of Peace'. As the worshippers slowly made their way to the church entrance, Mary stayed to listen to the organist's rendition of a prelude and fugue by J. S. Bach.

She felt renewed in her spirit and uplifted in her heart.

Didn't the pastor say in his sermon that Jesus came to heal the broken-hearted?

Mary was pleased she had come. Glancing once more round the chancel she got up from her seat and quietly walked out of the church, smiling at the vicar in his customary place at the door. She didn't stop, since he was busy talking to a group of well-hatted ladies clamouring for his attention. He glanced over their heads at Mary and smiled back. His eyes had a familiar look she thought, but dismissed the idea as fanciful.

There was a warm breeze in the air as Mary walked back to her cottage. Arriving home she ate a light snack and then settled down to read the book Isabel had lent her.

Opening the pages Mary couldn't help thinking what an apt title Brian had given to his book. Gordon was certainly unconscious of his behaviour.

She started to read:

> The person with a dementing illness cannot grasp learning situations as before because brain tissue has been damaged or destroyed. It is unrealistic, therefore, to expect the sufferer to learn new skills or even perform old ones in the same way; although their intellectual abilities are not lost all at once.
>
> Confused people ask the same questions again and again. Reassure them that you will take care of things. Respond-

ing with annoyance or attempting to argue doesn't help matters. Respond with warm affection to the pleasant things the person does, and ignore the annoying behaviour.

Mary rested the book in her lap for a moment, and remembered how upset she sometimes got when Gordon asked, "Who are you?" and "What are you doing in my house?"

Aston Wills, who had been a frequent visitor to Mary's home during Gordon's illness, advised her, "Just explain that you are his wife. If he persists ignore the question as if you hadn't heard it. Eventually he will stop asking the question. Distraction, not confrontation is the most sensible way of dealing with confused behaviour, and the wandering and aggression which arise from it."

Mary found it difficult and distressing at times, but eventually learnt how to cope and to avoid conflicting situations. Gordon was, after all, her husband and needed all the love and support she could give.

Some things are learned only in the "fiery furnace" and Mary knew this well enough.

She continued reading:

A person with a dementing illness cannot take responsibility for their own safety because they are no longer able to evaluate the consequences the way most of us do.

This means you have to lock away dangerous tools, sharp objects, solvents, paint, cleaning materials, buttons, the hot water system and medication. Move household furniture around as little as possible.

Dementia is a progressive decline in brain function, especially memory and intellect, so the patient will be forgetful and confused, and may have difficulty finding their way around the house. Mobility is very precious in the elderly; falling may lead to major injuries and fractures, so every precaution should be taken to minimise the risks.

Mary glanced at the time, ordered a taxi to take her to the hospital, and after cutting some flowers from her overgrown garden, was soon on her way to the hospital to see her husband.

Gordon acknowledged Mary's presence and this cheered her up; he seemed to like the flowers she had brought and Mary talked to him about his day, but he did not remember any part of it. She made an effort to talk to him about Kathleen, their home, the garden and the neighbours, but it was no use; it was a one way conversation. Her heart sank as she realised the significance of Gordon's withdrawal.

Mary stayed on for another half-an-hour and then after making him comfortable she kissed him tenderly, and left.

As she was leaving, the sister in charge of the ward came towards her and said, "Mrs Whittacker, I thought you might like to listen to this tape; it's from the radio programme 'Analysis of the Mind'. You may find it helpful. I wouldn't be too concerned about some of the terminology, just get the gist of what the speaker is saying."

Arriving home Mary made some tea, switched on the tape recorder, and settled down in her favourite chair to listen to the tape the nurse had given her.

The moment she heard the voice of the speaker she sat up and paid attention.

"My contribution to your very interesting programme about the human mind is to speak about confused behaviour, as families have shared their experiences with me, and hopefully to throw some light on the disturbance of consciousness."

"Well, this young man certainly gets around," said Mary out loud.

> What I have to say is not a substitute for professional skills. If illness of the mind and dementia in particular is suspected, one should consult a GP or a psychiatrist.
>
> Human consciousness has developed in a process that has taken aeons of time; this evolution is by no means complete. Large areas of the mind are still shrouded in mystery.
>
> In my talk today it is my intention to show how "misty"

consciousness determines certain kinds of behaviour – the kind which carers face each day, and which cause them so much stress and concern.

I don't think this programme is the platform for discussing the various theories of the levels of consciousness – the conscious, pre-conscious, the unconscious, and their attributes, so I'll leave these contentions aside.

Consciousness alters when substances such as drugs or alcohol are consumed past a sensible intake, affecting sensory perception of time, space and body awareness.

Those parts of the brain responsible for perception are disorganised following the assimilation of drugs and alcoholic beverages. If these are taken in large quantities the consciousness is altered to such a degree that reason and things of beauty are distorted in the process of perception.

In these altered states the consciousness, though not altogether diminished, may not receive the correct signals. Behaviour cannot be governed by good intentions or a balanced view. As sunlight is hindered from shining clearly through a dirty window, so the reasoning faculty is dimmed, resulting in confused behaviour.

A person's actions become confused when they are no longer performed under the objective awareness by which we know things, for example through the receptor senses – seeing, hearing, feeling, tasting and smelling. Also lacking will be the subjective consciousness, which is concerned with reasoning, imagination and abstract thinking.

When human consciousness is altered, as is the case in those whose perception of reality is obscured, we fail to recognise familiar people and things because the brain is not able to put the information together properly. It's a baffling symptom. In a sense the mind is blind.

Occasionally, however the long-term memory may be triggered and the patient responds positively, by a kind and familiar act.

Often carers are alone in the house with a relative suffering from dementia. The most appropriate action a carer can take during moments of confused and disturbed behaviour is evasive action. Try to divert attention to something positive and beautiful. If this fails and episodes of disturbed behaviour continue, chemotherapy may have to be introduced in consultation with the family doctor or psychiatrist.

Mary sensed a long pause in Brian's delivery; she waited to hear what he would say next.

My own pet theory is that consciousness may be found in every cell of the body and not isolated in any one part, such as the brain.

Human consciousness has far more to it than science and psychology can teach us. There is for instance awareness of God's Spirit, which human consciousness cannot discern unless God Himself bestows it upon a person.

> When God puts His Spirit in those who believe He makes it possible for us to go beyond the range of human thought, the orderliness of the universe, and discern the things of the spirit – which belong in another realm of consciousness.

The taped programme ended with Brian saying, "You will save yourself a lot of pain if you remember that your confused relative cannot make sense of what the eyes see. This is not a rejection of you, but an inexplicable confusion of the brain."

Mary remained seated in her chair trying to understand all she had heard. Suddenly there was a knock on the back door.

The only person to call using the rear entrance was Claire, Kelly's daughter from next door. She would often pop in through the opening of the privet hedge after school was over, especially when jam tarts were being made! Mary would listen to all she had to say and would reassure her when confidences were shared.

At weekends Claire would often spend time talking with Gordon when he was working in the garden. He would tell her the names of the plants and she would ask lots of questions as they sat in a shady spot near the rhododendrons at the bottom of the garden.

Claire's mother Kelly was a single parent and worked

part-time as a school teacher, so Mary often stood in as an adopted granny to Claire. They were good friends.

"Come and sit here," said Mary, pointing to the chair nearest to her, "and tell me what you've been doing."

When she was seated Claire reached into the pocket of her school blazer and pulled out a grubby piece of paper.

"I've written a poem for Uncle Gordon," she said, unfolding the paper, "because I want him to feel better."

Mary took the paper from Claire and began to read.

I don't see you in your garden; I can't play there any more,
The seeds, which we planted, look very sick and poor.
Please come home, Uncle Gordon, and fix my garden swing,
It doesn't work like it used to; I know you can do anything.
There's so much I want to tell you. I've got more A's this year,
And I'm cycling all the way to school, 'cos the fare is very dear.
Can you be home for my birthday? I have a surprise or two;
You'll love them, I know you will. I made them especially for you.

I do hope you're feeling better, it's my very greatest wish,
So please come home and see us – sealed with a loving kiss.

Claire

Mary sat with tears in her eyes, realising how Gordon had loved this little girl as a father; the times they spent in the garden chatting to each other had left an impression on her young mind.

Looking up at Claire Mary held out her arms, embraced her frail form and whispered, "You are your mother's child. She loves you and I love you; she will never let you down and nor will I; she will always be there for you, and I will always be your friend."

Claire's eyes shone as she kissed Mary and brushed back her hair. She then sat down to watch television. "Your mother will be home in half an hour," said Mary, as she went into the kitchen to fetch Claire some of the jam tarts which she had made earlier. These were soon devoured.

Outside, the sound of car doors being shut told Claire her mother had returned and it was time to go.

"Mum's home," Claire shouted. "Thanks! Love you." And she was gone.

FIVE

Mary wanted to understand a little more about Gordon's illness and so she resumed reading the book Isabel had lent her.

Why should anyone get Alzheimer's disease? This is a question which is often asked. To be perfectly honest I cannot give a satisfactory answer. Throughout my ministry I have tried to replace pessimism and helplessness, where I find it, with fresh hope and new optimism.

Research has shown that chemicals in the brain called neuro-transmitters are necessary for messages to pass from one nerve cell to another. It would seem that people with Alzheimer's disease have a deficiency of certain enzymes which produce the neuro-transmitter acetylcholine;

Nutritional deficiency, genetic factors, structural brain changes, a defective immune system and absorption of metals such as aluminium, have all to be considered as possible causes.

Another question often asked is, "Where is God when I pray to him, when I need Him? Doesn't He care what happens to me? He always seems a million miles away."

The greatest test for anyone who believes in the power of prayer is to live with God's silence. The Christian message is that faith in Him will not go unrewarded. His Word is true and will last for ever. So the secret is not to listen to His silence, but to look for His grace, which is present in abundance.

People need to know that God loves them with all their faults and failings. The common view is that God is far removed from our personal needs, silent to our cries for help. But this is not what His Word says.

"Have I not commanded you? Be strong and of good courage; do not be afraid, nor be dismayed, for the Lord your God is with you wherever you go." So be strong and of good courage!

Our Christian life is based on redemption, so as we pray God's Word over our circumstances He is bound by His promises to answer our prayers: "for everyone who asks receives." But in God's timing – and that is what is often so hard for us to bear.

We do not know why there should be suffering. Is it to do with the Fall as outlined in Genesis? Anyone who can explain suffering has obviously never suffered. Suffering is a fact of life, but it is more tolerable when the heart is right with God.

Suffering is harder to bear when, through self-love and an independent spirit, we refuse to submit either to God or nobler motives; though the world will tell you it's OK to do otherwise.

The God we Christians worship has a Father's heart; He is Someone who knows about suffering. He was Himself despised, rejected of men, and suffered the most awful grief and sorrow.

Suffering is nearly always the way to the holy ground. In the process something dies and no man is the same afterwards; either he is better or worse.

Mary laid aside the book. She had not been able to understand everything she had read, but somehow felt that by some strange turn of events, help and knowledge were to hand. She set about preparing supper.

Kathleen would be home shortly. She had been away attending a short course updating her computer and human resources management skills.

When Mary heard her daughter call out as she entered the front door she sighed with relief that Kathleen was home safely.

"What a journey!" Kathleen gasped, as she let her suitcase fall to the floor in the hall,"I've never known so much traffic on the roads."

She flopped into a comfortable chair and kicked off her shoes. Mary brought her in a welcome drink.

Both mother and daughter talked until midnight, then said goodnight.

Sleep did not come easily for Kathleen that night. Her

head was buzzing with terms like transactional analysis, therapeutic continuum, force-field analysis, dynamics of pastoral care, multimedia PC, floppy disk drives and so on.

The following day Kathleen visited her father at Coopersfield. Standing beside the bed and just about to leave, was the tall figure of James Brookes, assigned to the hospital whilst the usual chaplain was indisposed.

"Hello," he beamed. "I was just talking with Gordon about how electronics have changed during these past few years; he is quite knowledgeable."

Kathleen glanced at her father. She had noticed that he was responding to the chaplain's conversation. How was it that a total stranger could engage his attention in this way? Was his long-term memory still intact?

The tall clergyman and Kathleen exchanged greetings and she learned that he had the same surname as Brian.

"It's nice to see you again, and I'm delighted that the other business ended satisfactorily for you. You will want to have some time alone with your father, so I'll say goodbye for the time being."

Turning to Gordon he said gently, "I'll look in to see you again." Kathleen saw him speaking to other patients on the way out.

She watched him for a while. He certainly cut a fine

figure, and she felt good about meeting him. Here was someone who was able to reach her father – not as a patient, but as a human being.

Kathleen sat with her father, talking about her childhood days, until she saw him nodding off, and reassuring him she left. On her way home Kathleen thought of something her father had said just before his illness: "A young person should be able to embrace life; an older one to bid farewell to it."

She wondered if he was thinking about that now. He once told her never to be surprised at anyone's behaviour, nor at what happens. He believed that we all carry within ourselves the seeds of the unpredictable, often without our knowledge, so we can't afford to be complacent about anything, nor too quick to judge another human being.

Kathleen arrived home to find her mother seated at the piano; it was here that Mary found solace and fresh inspiration. She looked up as her daughter entered, wondering again if she secretly loved this Brian of hers. If she did she did not say.

"I think it's time to invite your friend to dinner again, don't you?" said Mary. She thought she saw a slight blush on Kathleen's face as she spoke.

"Well, yes, that's a good idea. Don't forget he's bringing someone with him," Kathleen reminded her.

"We'll send the invitation off today." Mary was feeling pleased with herself. She was hoping to be on form to entertain her guests.

The days passed quickly and the night of the dinner came. Everything was ready and Mary called out, "They will be here soon."

At that moment the doorbell sounded. Putting the finishing touches to her hair, Kathleen skipped across the hall and opened the door.

At Brian's side stood James Brookes. Kathleen's eyes almost popped out of her head. She stood aside to let them in as Mary came forward with her hand extended. She intended this evening to be successful. It was just what was needed in Primrose Cottage – the company of charming men.

"Ah, Brian," she beamed. Then Mary caught sight of those green eyes. Brian seemed to be enjoying the look of amazement on Kathleen's and Mary's face.

"This is my father," said Brian. "Of course," Kathleen murmured, then hurriedly correcting herself, she managed to say, "We have met."

Jimmy Brookes smiled. "I'm honoured that you should invite me, considering this is a difficult time for you."

"Come in and have a drink," replied Mary. The two men followed Mary into the living room. "What can I get you?"

"I'll be content with an orange juice for the moment, please," replied Jimmy Brookes.

"So will I," Brian added.

"I thought you were bringing a friend," Kathleen whispered to Brian.

"So I have," he replied. "He might be my father, but he's also my friend and mentor. I couldn't have better."

Glancing between Brian and his father Kathleen could see the resemblance. "That's a most unusual relationship," declared Kathleen.

"He's a very unusual man," Brian whispered back.

"Let's eat," said Mary after they had finished chatting.

Mary was a good cook, and her guests were enjoying themselves. "It really is kind of you to organise this evening," said Jimmy, leaning towards his hostess. "I can't remember when I've enjoyed a meal so much."

Mary smiled and turning to Brian said, "I'd like your opinion about something. Do you think there will ever be a cure for dementia?"

Brian thought for a moment, and Kathleen sensed his passion for getting his facts right and making himself understood.

"Since dementia involves the irreversible degeneration of brain tissue and a consequent loss of intellectual function, the treatments available to relieve these symptoms are at best limited. I wish I could be more hopeful.

But research continues and, who knows, perhaps one day there will be a breakthrough."

Kathleen, almost assuming the role of his former student said, "Alzheimer's involves the loss of certain brain cells, resulting in the development of minute 'plaques' in the brain, doesn't it?"

"That's correct," Brian responded. "There is some hope that in the future certain medicines and even surgery, which might involve neural transplants, could be developed which will reduce the number of people suffering from Alzheimer's disease."

"Well, hurrah for that day," Kathleen exclaimed.

There was silence for a few moments, then Brian's father spoke, slowly and deliberately. "I think our world is in need of a new medicine which combines knowledge, compassion and the spirit in the process of recovery and healing. Clinicians are busy people, but it might help if they spend some time with patients, before and after an operation, listening to what they have to say."

"How will compassion help to alleviate the pain from something like a pathogenic virus?" asked Kathleen.

"What's a pathogenic virus?" Mary enquired.

Kathleen responded quickly to alleviate her mother's concern. "It simply means 'disease producing,' Mother."

Jimmy Brookes went on, "Not all germs are our

deadly enemy. Some are bound up in the DNA which is at the centre of an entire information network called our immune system. Like the wheat and the chaff, they need to be recognised for what they are and dealt with, though the body-cellular make-up is well equipped to take care of most of the "chaff".

"The immune system, like the brain, has an enormous capacity for absorbing new information, learning and memorising the identity of any diseased organism. Both the brain and the immune system operate within the same chemical network, however."

"This is interesting," said Mary excitedly. "Tell us more."

"Nerve pathways exist between the brain and the furthest parts of the body," Jimmy continued. "Along these pathways travel 'chemical messengers' called neuro-transmitters. They act as 'communicator molecules' as their name implies, and transmit nerve impulses. In effect, the neurones of the brain 'talk' to the rest of the body, touching the life of every cell."

"Can you give us an example?" Kathleen enquired.

"Neuro-transmitters each have their own molecular structure," he replied, "and a different message to deliver. In our sleep and waking patterns, for example, the body is aroused in the morning by a series of time signals, at first mild and then stronger as we are wakened from a deep sleep by stages. It's a gradual process, from the biochemistry of sleep, to the biochemistry of wakefulness."

There was silence for a few moments then, addressing his father, Brian said, "There is much that has gone unexplained about pain and how we deal with it."

"Our tolerance to pain depends on the body's ability to regulate the sensation of pain as, for example, when a wounded soldier fights on, or when a parent rushes into a burning house to rescue a child. Both are able to ignore the pain of their injuries.

"The pain threshold in all of us rises and falls according to the human spirit and the ability of body-proteins, which repair cells, build new ones, heal cuts and bruises and so on. The body is no small miracle."

Jimmy Brookes was thoughtful for a moment, then said, "The mind is superior to matter. When both the mind and spirit, together with the body-chemicals, such as endorphins, peptides, and messenger molecules, work in harmony, masterminded by DNA, this helps to bring about a speedy healing process. There are many variables, of course, but nothing moves in the body without moving the whole. If one part of the immune system is disturbed, the body feels it in numerous places. It's a wonderfully designed interactive communicative network. And there I rest my case," he finished laughingly.

"Wow! What an evening," exclaimed Mary.

"It isn't finished yet," Kathleen responded.

"Why, what do you mean?" her mother asked.

"There's something very important we've overlooked."

"There's perhaps a lot we've overlooked," joked Brian.

"All this talk about science is great, but where does God fit into this analysis? I may not understand all of God's Word, but it does have something to say about the creation of us human beings."

Jimmy Brookes was the first to speak. "Well done, Kathleen. We get so caught up in our neat divisions of body, nervous system, endocrine system, digestive system and so on, and how the neuro-chemicals influence the whole of the body, that we overlook a medicine which is much older than Hippocrates. God's Word also has an influence on our health, as it says in the Book of Proverbs: 'For they are life to those who find them, and healing to all their flesh.'

"Through the messenger-molecules, the body is made aware of what is happening to its various parts. Each messenger is a strand in the body's web of intelligence. Touch one and the whole web quivers, relating messages to other parts of the body. God is at work in all this."

Mary beamed with satisfaction as the conversation flowed from neuro-chemicals to immune cells, to the workings of God. Gordon's illness had brought a cloud of sadness over Primrose Cottage, and Mary was sick at heart that her husband could no longer share her life in the home they had built together. This was a special evening for her, and took away some of the pain.

She looked over at her daughter, smiling, radiant and beautiful; she seemed attracted to the young minister, but there appeared no obvious response from his green eyes, save a warm friendliness.

The conversation had subsided, and Brian said, "Father, I think it's time we should be going," adding with a mischievous smile, "and you can finally rest your case."

"You are absolutely right, my son. Mary, you have been a most gracious hostess. Thank you."

"Thanks for your hospitality, Mary," beamed Brian as they prepared to leave.

"You must come again," Mary said, returning his smile.

Kathleen showed them to the door, and Mary returned to the living room satisfied that the evening had gone well.

MARY

SIX

It was Kathleen's day off. She was gazing through her window watching the rain make patterns on the glass. Her marriage to Robert had been so short lived, and she had hardly had time to get to know him before the accident which took his life and left her alone, without a lover. In her mind she heard the familiar voice of her father speaking to her needs.

"One day you will fall in love, and you will know when it happens. Love is the greatest thing we can receive from anyone, and it's the most we can give to others. All too often we let the harsh realities of life prevent us from responding to the love of those around us; we sometimes fail to grasp the friendly hand extended towards us."

"Now more than ever she needed to hear her father's words of wisdom. She gave a sigh and the child in her cried out, "Oh, Daddy, why did you have to go and catch this awful illness? I need you so." As she wept silently she heard again the gentle voice of her father: "Contentment isn't getting what we want but being satisfied with what we have. Very often dreams are all we have to keep us going."

Kathleen recalled reading something like that in the Bible, written by the apostle Paul: "I have learned in whatever state I am to be content."

The following weeks passed quickly. Gordon showed little signs of recovery, although he was allowed up occasionally.

Early one morning, as Mary was resting in her wicker chair, the telephone rang.

"I'll get it," Kathleen called out. There was a long silence, and then Mary heard Kathleen say, "We'll be over right away."

Both Mary and Kathleen hurried to the hospital after hearing that Gordon's physical health was deteriorating.

Mary remained at Gordon's side, while Kathleen went off to find the ward sister for her prognosis. After a short discussion, the sister said, "It has happened so fast. It seems unlikely that he will recover. I am sorry."

Kathleen returned to her mother, who was holding Gordon's hand and crying quietly.

"Oh, Kathleen," she cried. "Oh, Kathy." Mary and Kathleen were locked in each other's arms when the sister came to check on Gordon.

"He's asleep at the moment," Mary managed to say through her tears.

"He's gone," the sister said quietly.

"Stay here. I'll be back in few moments." Kathleen quickly made a phone call to Brian. But he was not available and she had no means of contacting him. At that moment James Brookes walked into the ward, and seeing Kathleen said, "I knew you would have need of me."

Kathleen looked at him intently and wondered what sort of man he was. He certainly had an uncanny sense of timing.

As they approached Gordon's bedside, Mary was sobbing quietly. James laid his hands on Mary's shoulder and said gently, "Human life and sorrow are partners until we know how to attune to the divine will."

He remained standing at her side and prayed, "Father in heaven, eternal Lord, bestow upon these your children, the Spirit of your love, so they may be in harmony with your divine will and at peace with themselves.

"Oh, Thou unchanging Lord, grant to the soul of your servant the peace which passes all understanding. In your love and mercy Lord, accept him into your kingdom, where he will know the glories of heaven with you and the saints for ever.

"We praise your holy name that the precious blood of Jesus has ransomed Gordon. And now, trusting in the promises of your Son, we commend him to your merciful keeping. Amen."

Turning to Mary, he said, "Gordon's soul is at peace. God will honour His word. Try to accept this glorious truth, Mary, and death will lose its power to cause you pain."

Then lowering his voice he quoted some words from the author of Romans, "None of us live to ourselves and none of us die to ourselves."

Kathleen looked on silently. Who was this man who could speak with such healing balm? His words possessed none of the theological dogma used by so many in the church.

Addressing Kathleen, James Brookes said with calm assurance, "Your father has cut his last cord of attachment to this material world, and has gone to his ever-living identity in the Spirit. He has gone home, to be with the Lord."

With a final word of reassurance for Mary, James Brookes disappeared through the door of Ward 12.

Once home, Kathleen made her mother comfortable for the night, and then braced herself to think about the funeral arrangements.

The following morning, as Mary was resting in her wicker chair on the small patio, Kathleen called out to her mother, "There's someone here to see you."

Mary turned to see Brian walking towards her. He waited a few moments then sat beside her in a vacant chair. Neither spoke for a while, then almost in a whisper, Mary said, "There's something grotesque about death. It has a faceless mask, I hate it!"

She continued to stare ahead, looking at but not seeing Gordon's garden now overgrown and untidy.

Brian waited. Mary continued, almost talking to herself, "It's the king of terrors," she murmured, quoting the Book of Job, "an open wound to the living."

Still Brian remained silent. He knew from long experience that a person in grief doesn't need logical reasoning, so he just sat there and listened. After a time, Mary said, "Talk to me."

"Death is the supreme enigma. What we don't understand, we often fear," he commented quietly. "Losing someone we love is hard to bear. In the scriptures death is described as 'the enemy' – 'the last enemy to be destroyed'. It's in the matrix of creation that wounds eventually heal, then we can go forward in the joyous hope of reunion, when God calls us home."

Mary continued to stare out at the garden, though she was listening carefully to all Brian had to say. Sensing that Mary wished to be alone, he quietly withdrew.

She closed her eyes and saw the garden as it used to be. The dozens of candelabra primulas, which had spread like a purple carpet alongside the oval-shaped pond in the shadows of the magnolia and lilac. Mary was very fond of the candelabra variety, with their flowers balanced delicately on the stems.

The privet hedge had always been neatly trimmed, but now had unruly stems pointing in all directions. The lawn was blighted with moss, lichen and other weeds.

The afternoon sun shone down on Mary as she continued to reflect. Then, in the distance, she heard the sound of the Blue Danube waltz, which Kathleen had turned on. Mary remembered how she and Gordon had waltzed together. She dozed peacefully for the next hour or so.

Claire's voice from over the garden gate stirred Mary from her snooze. There was something special about this girl, and Mary suddenly felt protective towards her. "Oh, Claire come and tell me what you've been doing since I last saw you."

Claire seated herself next to Mary and, reaching inside the pocket of her school blazer, she took out a neatly folded piece of paper. "I've written a poem for Uncle Gordon," she said, as she unfolded the paper and handed it to Mary. "I've called it 'A Childhood Memory'."

Mary took the paper from Claire and without saying a word began to read:

A Childhood Memory

In your lovely garden away from my school,
You spoke to me of flowers and of nature's golden rule.
And from a bough of our tree where birds loved to sing,
You hung two thick strands of rope and made a garden swing.

I watched you work among your ferns,
Dotted about in a mosaic of turns.
The day you built the old stone wall,
I cried because I'd lost my ball.

One day you found it among the flowers,
As you were whistling 'April showers.'
I liked your pond where dragon-flies meet,
You were always saying it was very deep.

From my open window late at night,
I heard frogs croak on their breeding site.
Among your plant pots sprouting new leaves,
A blackbird built his nest with ease.

The tawny owl still hoots as he swoops past,
I caught a glimpse of it the night before last.
I hope you still have a garden, set in radiant hue,
With lovely flowers which give out sweet fragrance too.

I'll always remember your kindness, your gentle loving ways,
You help build fond memories of my childhood days.

May the garden in your new home be one which all can
share,
But most all may it be where you can sit, in
contemplative prayer.
I love you. Claire

Mary was holding back tears as she said to Claire, "Darling, never give up writing. It's a lovely poem, may I keep it, please?"

"I want you to have it," replied Claire, pleased that Mary liked it.

"I must go now. Mummy's home," Claire said. She gave Mary a hug, and skipped across the lawn through the privet hedge gate.

The shock of Gordon's death had left Mary feeling quite numb; yet she acknowledged the help and support she was receiving, and silently thanked her new friends before going to bed that night.

The following morning during breakfast, Mary said to Kathleen, "I would like Brian to conduct the funeral service."

"I thought you might," she answered. "I've already asked him."

"Thank you, dear," Mary responded.

"I have to go now. Will you be all right?" Kathleen called.

"Of course I will," Mary answered.

As the morning progressed, Mary was beginning to feel much better. Suddenly the door bell rang. "Who can this be?" Mary thought to herself.

Standing on the doorstep looking very elegant was the Rev'd James Brookes.

"Jimmy!" Mary exclaimed. "This is an unexpected joy. Do come in. It's nice to see you."

"I don't wish to intrude," he smiled, "but this is the only chance I may have to call."

"It's a lovely morning, let's sit out here." Leading her new friend out on to the veranda and finding him a seat, she excused herself and went indoors to fetch some drinks.

Within a few minutes Mary was once again looking into those green eyes which so captivated his listeners. "I am so glad you were there at the hospital, Gordon's death was a great shock, though I had expected it."

Jimmy Brookes let Mary talk, and talk she did. She told him of the guilt she felt at leaving Gordon in hospital and how she felt cheated because she had not been able to celebrate their Ruby Wedding anniversary.

"I saw all this coming when we had the shop and Gordon became so forgetful. Often he would not open for business, but go and sit by the river. When I asked him about his day, he couldn't remember anything about it. It wasn't until I called in to see him and looked at the accounts that I realised how serious things were. I should have acted before, and maybe none of this would have happened, and we would still be together." With that she burst into tears.

Jimmy Brookes knew that the closer we are to God, the closer we are bound to our neighbour, so he listened carefully to all that Mary had to say as she opened her heart and poured out her troubles. When she had been silent for a while, he leaned forward and said in a gentle voice, "Mary, in this life we are born to trouble. It's part of our environment and no one escapes it. Indeed, the Bible teaches that it's part of our birthright. I suppose we all desire to live long, yet not grow old, but every phase of life prepares us for the one to follow.

"We don't all age in the same way, but our bodies more than our minds age in common patterns.

"Old age is rich in possibilities: to unlearn the follies of a lifetime, to see through inbred self-deception, to deepen our understanding and compassion, and rid ourselves of prejudice and the vested interests that thwart the spirit.

"So, Mary, be filled with the Spirit which fills the earth around you, and as you spend more time with Him, His light will shine on you and fill your heart with His peace."

He paused, as if waiting for inspiration, and then said, "Does a seed die because it's buried in the earth? Hidden within our sorrows there is often a blessing. Try not to miss it. Now, if you'll excuse me, I must be going."

Mary thanked him for his visit and James Brookes walked off into the sunshine. Mary never saw him again. She felt that she had entertained an angel, who had opened her mind to the truth of the Scriptures.

A short time after he had gone, Mary was deep in thought about the events of the past weeks. How strange, she reflected, that these two men had turned up just as she was in need of help and wise counsel. And there was Isobel Adams. All three in their own way had spoken words of comfort into her life, yet she hardly knew them. Mary felt an inner strength rise up within her.

Although she didn't attend church as much as some others in the village, she believed that God is everywhere and that His love is broader than the measure of man's mind.

She silently thanked God for Gordon's release from the "unseen intruder" and asked for strength to cope with the coming days.

Mary sat in her favourite chair thinking of Gordon. She prayed for the gift of rest in heaven for a weary soul. Then, through the mist of her grief, she thought she heard the voice of her husband say, "Turn again to life, and don't be sad or have tears of regret. For the sake of the memories we've shared, turn to life and smile."

Mary rose from her seat and went to a small cupboard in her bedroom; she pulled out a wooden box inlaid with spring flowers which contained some letters and love notes from Gordon. The dreaded curse of Gordon's illness began to fade from her thoughts as she read his scribbled love notes, which she had so often found on her pillow or dressing table, in her jacket pocket or up the sleeve of a raincoat. She had kept them carefully over the years.

"I love you, sweetheart. I love you for what you are, and for what I am when I am with you."

"I love you for helping me become what I am, and for the many tender ways you do things for me."

"I love you, dearest one, for being my wife, my lover and my friend."

"Every time I am parted from you, I die a little."

"Because of your love for me, each day becomes more blest because you care."

"If any one thing has helped me through the years, it is your love for me; such love has softened the selfishness of my desires."

"When my courage failed this morning, your words of love held me up. Thank you, darling."

"When the time comes for us to part, and you are feeling lonely and sick at heart, release your sorrow through tears, and cherish the memories of our happy years."

Mary carefully replaced Gordon's love notes in the box again, and quietly cried herself to sleep in her wicker chair.

The day of the funeral came. Mary had received many cards expressing sympathy. Both Kathleen and Isobel escorted Mary to the little church on the hill, where Brian conducted a brief but dignified service for Gordon.

Brian spoke of Gordon's compassion for people and nature, his love and knowledge of flowers and gardening, and of his accomplishments as Chairman of Cowley Down Horticultural Society. He spoke also of the bond of friendship between him and Mary.

With a warm glance at Mary, Brian said, "Such love does not end in the grave."

In a fleeting moment Kathleen's eyes met Brian's. His words are like silken threads woven from heart to heart, she thought to herself.

The service ended with the hymn, "The day thou gavest, Lord, is ended."

With the words of the hymn in her ears, Mary, with Kathleen and her friends, followed Brian and the coffin bearers to the graveside. As Brian was saying the final words, Mary's resolute spirit gave way and she burst into tears. At that moment, the thick veil which had covered her senses was torn from her mind, and she remembered Jimmy's words, "Does a seed die because it is buried in the earth?"

Brian had finished. Taking one last look at the coffin in the ground, Mary murmured to herself, "Give to the earth what belongs to the earth, and to God that which belongs to God." She had hardly uttered these words when a ray of sunshine fell across the coffin.

As they were leaving, Mary looked up and saw Aston standing quietly in the background. He said nothing, but his presence filled Mary's soul with appreciation of all that he had done.

SEVEN

The events of the past months had stirred Mary's spirit from its slumbers, and she was beginning to appreciate all that God was doing in her life. She realised that He was not a remote and distant deity wrapped in mystical obscurity, but a living God who cared for His children.

She reflected how blind she had been to His presence and how conditioned to live by her own five fallible senses. It began to dawn on her that the Creator of the universe was her Father, her Friend, and the source of her faith.

He had touched her life at many turns, and spoken to her in subtle and sensitive ways by His gentle Holy Spirit, and lately through the ministry of James, Brian, Isobel and Claire.

She felt an enormous gratitude for His generosity. She began to discover a fresh relationship with Him as her Father. It was as if He had put a new spirit within her and her soul cried out, "Bless the Lord, O my soul, and all that is within me, bless His holy name."

In her heart Mary knew that she loved God because He had first loved her; and in that precious moment it became clear to her that God honours humble faith with innumerable benefits and remarkable blessings.

The cloud of Gordon's illness was lifted from Primrose Cottage, and Mary set about putting things in order. She engaged the services of Jim, a local gardener to make her gardens ready for next spring.

Isobel had remained with Mary for a few days after the funeral and during that time had confided in Mary that she was not able to commit herself to Christianity, because she didn't understand it.

"Have you never read the Gospels?" asked Mary.

"I have tried to read them," Isobel replied, "but they remain a mystery to me, can you explain them?"

Mary laughed. "I wish I could, but I'll tell you this . . ."

And for the next hour the Holy Spirit loosened Mary's tongue to speak eloquently of Christ and why He had come in human flesh to subject Himself to the frailties and temptations of humanity. Mary spoke of how Jesus remained a spotless lamb to be sacrificed for the salvation of mankind.

As Mary was speaking, the Holy Spirit fell on her, and she began to praise Him in a language she had never used before. Isobel, too, felt the Spirit of God touch her, and under the anointing of God she gave her heart to the Lord.

"O Mary, I feel so wonderful," Isobel cried out. "A peace I've never known before." Mary and Isobel embraced in a loving hug, as God's Holy Spirit filled them with His power, and the two women prayed for a world in need.

Mary was mindful of the scripture which says, "If two of you agree on earth concerning anything they ask, it will be done for them by my Father in heaven." Her spirit called out within her, "Two are better than one because they have a good reward for their labour; for if they fall, one will lift up their companion."

Both Mary and Isobel gave heed to the move of the Spirit and faith filled their souls.

In the medical ward of Coopersfield Hospital some miles away, Kathleen was preparing to end her duties for the day. The psychiatric department was just two floors up, and there Brian was completing his rounds. When he had finished, he put away his papers, closed his office door and made his way to the main entrance.

As he walked down the stairs his thoughts were of Kathleen. They had known each other for a long time. They had laughed and joked about their work, enjoyed many a heated debate; he had shared her grief and sorrows, and was only now beginning to realise that he was in love with her. "How could I have been so blind," he said out loud to himself.

Did he have the strength to commit himself again to the love of a woman? It was not that his nature was without love. But how and why love is awakened, he could not tell. Was it that Kathleen had released some secret spring of love in the depths of his being? Perhaps love comes on the heels of knowledge and grows out of friendship.

It had not been for him a question of love at first sight, which seemed to his analytical mind quite incomprehensible and unreasonable, even though it happened to others.

Brian was aware that it was God's plan to make us dependent on one another for the inspiration, the stimulation and the joys which prevent life from becoming monotonous. As he approached the foot of the stairs he resolved to tell Kathleen at the first opportunity how he felt.

As he walked out into the sunshine a familiar voice said, "Hello!"

Brian looked over his shoulder. Kathleen was standing there, smiling at him. "I was just on my way home," she said.

"Well . . . do you have to rush?" Brian stammered. Kathleen thought he lacked his usual composure and she recalled her father saying to her one day as they sat chatting in the garden, "When a man is first in love, he shows timidity and sometimes awkwardness."

What has happened to him, she mused. "No, I'm in no hurry," she answered.

"Let's go for a walk," he suggested.

Kathleen consented, and went forward hearing the music of the angels. Could it be that she was going to hear what she had so longed for? She obeyed her natural instincts, to love and love always.

The sky was cloudless, and there was something in the unruffled calm of nature as Brian and Kathleen walked hand in hand down the leafy lanes. The peace of love healed the wounds of grief which had clung to her heart. She smiled as she heard the blackbird sing, and remembered her father quoting some words of Victor Hugo "Be like the bird, that pausing in her flight awhile on boughs too slight, feels them give way beneath her and yet sings, knowing that she has wings."

Kathleen leaned her head on Brian's shoulder as she felt his arm around her waist, and she knew at last that she had found the man with whom she would spend the rest of her life.

Autumn came and winter came. Although dead to this world Gordon was alive in Mary's heart and mind. She surrendered her will to the will of God and basked in her memories of the man who had made her the happiest woman in the world.

For the first time Aston Wills, who had faithfully monitored Gordon's mental health before his admission to hospital, and who had continued to visit Mary at her request, was at a loss. Mary's health was deteriorating. It seemed almost as though her love for Gordon drew her to his side in the world of spirit. Her doctors could find nothing physically wrong with her, but Mary pined for Gordon, as a youth pines for first love.

He recalled Mary describing her first meeting with Gordon. "The real wonder of love," she had said, "is that it can lift two ordinary people into a life that is extraordinary. We hear a great deal about unsuccessful marriages. Many couples make mistakes and quarrel over trifling things," she said sadly, "but I believe that when every husband stays a true lover, and every wife a sweetheart, love will remain in blossom."

"Is this what made your marriage a success?" Aston asked. Mary answered simply, "We were not victims of passion; I had a friend in my husband."

Although now very weak Mary invited Aston to call and see her, for what she called a "little chat"; she was very fond of his cheerful and funny ways, and enjoyed their conversations.

When he arrived she was sitting on the veranda in her favourite wicker chair.

She began by saying, "We built our marriage on what was written in that friendly letter which John sent out to the early church: 'There is no fear in love, for perfect love casts out fear.'

"Love and fear are spiritual forces. Gordon and I both tried to make sure that we walked with the right companion," she said smiling. Then her face brightened up as if she had received a revelation. "When we walk in love there is an unseen army of angels moving with us all the time. They are God's ministering spirits sent to help and protect us."

Mary saw the doubtful look on Aston's face and laughed. "You young people want so much proof. Read about it for yourself in the scriptures, in the letter called Hebrews. You'll find it in chapter one," she whispered.

He did so at the first opportunity. "Are they not all ministering spirits (angels) sent forth to minister for those who will inherit salvation?"

Aston sat gazing at Mary. She was the grandmother he never had. She was reclining in her wicker chair wrapped in the shawl given to her by her friend, Isobel Adams.

Glancing over the privet hedge, Aston saw the swing hanging idly from the tree next door. Mary had closed her eyes. He withdrew leaving her to rest. He never saw her again.

Mary died as she had lived, gazing upon the image of her husband. Her passing was peaceful, and according to her daughter almost angelic.

Aston attended Mary's funeral, which was taken by the new incumbent of the local parish church.

Kathleen had found Claire's poems and one that Mary herself had written. They were all under Mary's pillow. Hers was entitled, "The Faceless Mask". It read:

> O death, who gave you your sting,
> To inflict pain on everything?
> Is that your role in life's strange game,
> To remove everyone from their name?
> There will come a time when you will not escape,
> You will lose your power to cause pain and rape.
> O death, where then will be your sting?
> You will have no victory over anything.

Aston had known this remarkable woman for a short time only, yet he loved and respected her. Gordon had a loving heart which overflowed with kindness and zeal until his illness. Mary's heart had been so full of love that it passed beyond the measure of this life.

James Brookes, who had a great gift to calm troubled

waters, was called to another appointment. Isobel Adams, who had proved such a staunch friend, retired to Somerset. Young Claire with her mother moved to America, where she attained great distinction in literary circles.

Kathleen and Brian's love blossomed and they were married quietly in Cowley Down Parish church by the Rev'd James Brookes.

There were rumours among the villagers that Mary had lived in a world of fantasy; that she had heard and seen what no one else could see or hear.

Members of the Women's Institute remember an elderly curate, who had long since moved on, saying, "Mary lived for the most part in the realms of dreams, believing that the prophesies of Isaiah were words of wisdom composed in a book of precious stones, mounted on an altar of love, and that St John's visions were to be shared by those with spiritual insight."

Two of the "holy dusters" from St Andrew's, remembered Mary as the "kind lady at the cottage, always willing to donate flowers to decorate the church."

The church warden, Lady Bannington, said, "Mary was known in the village as that 'visionary woman'. Her eyes shone with kindness and love and her relationship with her husband was a song of peace, which soothed his mind when he was perplexed."

As Aston listened to the stories about this devoted couple, it dawned on him that life can be seen and experienced through the spirit, though the world around us is understood through reasoning, filled with sorrow and mingled with joy.

He began to wonder if the day would come when beauty, knowledge and virtue, would embrace scientific achievement and unite the human race.

In his more adventurous and creative moments he wanted to see the world as Mary was reputed to have seen it, with the eyes of the spirit, and grasp the secrets of what lies beyond the veil of human thought.

He recalled in one of his earlier interviews with Mary that he had asked her about the spirit. After making some notes at the time, he had put them aside with no further thought. Later he reflected that what she told him could not have come from reading about it, or from lectures on the subject, but from the Spirit Himself. He didn't understand it at the time.

This is how she explained it to him: "It all started in a garden. When man lived there he had a perfect relationship with God. His spirit was the dominant force in his life. Then sin came and the man was driven out of the garden, away from God's presence, to live dominated by his five senses – seeing, hearing, feeling, tasting, and smelling.

"The real man is a spirit being, but the moment his senses took charge, spiritual death occurred. In other words, he lost his approach to God the moment he sinned.

"When the man in the garden was disobedient, his nature changed and he became a stranger to himself. He was no longer dominated by the spirit, but by the body in which he lived.

"The brain is not able to think independently of sense evidence, so reasoning is dependent upon the senses; it has no contact with God who is Spirit. It's not until the human spirit is re-created – in other words receives the nature of God – that man's senses are made subject to the spirit again.

"One of the reasons why the Word of God is so often misunderstood is because the mind is blind; it must be renewed. We have to put the mind to work otherwise it stops learning. Remember, the brain gets exhausted when it does nothing!

"The Word of God is the work of the Holy Spirit. Sense knowledge is not able to understand spiritual things so we need to meditate on the Word, and ask God to put a new spirit in us.

"There is such a thing as the mind of the spirit, and a mind of the senses. The former leads to life and peace. The latter to spiritual death. Hence the term 'you must be born again'. When the spirit in us is renewed, we grow in knowledge beyond the reactions of our senses upon the brain.

"Have you ever been working hard on a problem, wrestling with it night and day, and then when you rested, exhausted by it all, suddenly the answer flashed across your mind? The moment your reasoning was switched off, the spirit was free to rise up and solve the problem.

"With your training you will want to believe it comes from the 'sub-conscious mind', but the truth is, it is the mind of the spirit struggling to express itself.

"When the human spirit is re-created it is brought into subjection to the Word of God. If we violate His Word the soul loses its joy and peace, and this may lead to discontentment. If we persist in disobedience the soul has a habit of doing those things which are not fitting, and we'll follow the lusts of the heart."

And there his notes ended.

It was many months before Aston passed by Primrose Cottage again. A "For Sale" notice was up, and the cottage was vacant. The sun was just setting and casting shadows on the rooftop and windows, and there was a strange stillness surrounding this corner of God's acre.

Mary had remained a faithful wife and friend to her husband, even when things became difficult. She was his strength, his eyes and ears, she cared for him when he needed her most. And when she was in need God sent His messengers to counsel her and set her mind at rest.

Now they are both beyond the sunset with the Lord and his angels, where the "silent enemy" has no jurisdiction.

To close this episode of my story I think Mary should have the last word: "Dementia has taken my husband's body, but it will not have his spirit."

ASTON WILLS

EIGHT

The country roads were quiet as Aston drove past the farms and isolated houses. The morning sun beamed across the fields and through the trees, penetrating the early morning mist. The air was fresh and cool. A rooster crowed in the distance. The beauty and peace of this countryside seemed to ease the long journey he had taken to be with the Rev'd Brian and Mrs Kathleen Brookes.

It would not be long now before he reached his destination. The ancient town of Bamford was just ahead. As he drove over a rustic bridge approaching this charming little town he could see a meadow to his left which appeared like a soft green blanket covering the rich soil of this unspoilt shire. A few friendly voices broke the stillness as he made his way slowly past the stone houses towards Briony Lodge, the home of Mary's daughter.

Entering the short but spacious driveway, he parked his car and walked towards the entrance of the house. Immediately the door was opened by the housekeeper, a woman in her mid-fifties, and Aston was shown to a seat in the hall. He hadn't been seated long when a slim, athletic young man burst through the door. It was Mary's grandson. He was tall and good looking, with the same green-blue eyes, and a smile that would melt the stoniest heart.

When he saw Aston sitting there, he came to an abrupt standstill, introduced himself and said, "Hello. You've driven a long way. I suppose you're here to see my parents."

Before Aston could reply the young man smiled and said, "I noticed the windscreen of your car is covered with flies and dirt, which indicates that you have travelled a long distance, probably using the motorway."

Aston nodded as the young man excused himself and disappeared through one of the doors off the hallway. So this was the son of Brian and Kathleen Brookes, Aston mused. He couldn't wait to meet them again.

Finally Kathleen and Brian came into the hall. "Please forgive our discourtesy for keeping you waiting," she said, as she approached him.

They both greeted him warmly. It was many years since they had last met but Kathleen was still beautiful and her husband elegant. What a perfect match, he thought to himself. He tried to recall Brian's age. He appeared to be in his forties, but Aston was sure that he was older than that. He remembered Mary saying, "A youthful appearance is a matter of a calm soul combined with a fine mind."

As he gazed at Kathleen, Aston had a strange feeling that her mother was looking at him; she had the same reassuring presence and those gentle eyes, which seemed to look right into the soul, not in a critical way, but with compassion.

Kathleen had matured into a graceful lady, and Aston couldn't help but recall how her romance had developed, especially after Mary's motherly intervention.

After exchanging friendly greetings, they went into Brian's study. The walls were piled high with books and his desk littered with papers. Brian noticed Aston gazing at a framed photograph.

"That's a picture of my father with the Bishop of London and some friends from India," he explained.

Kathleen excused herself, but soon returned with some light refreshments. "I hear you've met our son, Christopher," she remarked as she sat down beside her husband.

"He's a fine boy," Aston replied, "and very observant."

"Yes, he's that all right," added his father, smiling.

Kathleen said, "It really is good of you to come all this way to see us. My mother was very fond of you and appreciated all that you did for her and Daddy before they both went to sleep. My husband and I are most grateful. We'd like you to stay for lunch and meet our friends. I'll leave you two together for a while."

With that she left the room. Aston turned his attention to Brian. There was a gentleness mixed with an inner strength about his personality.

Without any preliminaries Brian asked, "Wills, have you ever considered offering yourself for the priesthood?"

"I did when I was young," he replied.

"Any reason why you didn't pursue it?" Brian enquired.

"None serious," Aston reflected. "I took an interest in mental health and psychology, and have remained in that field ever since."

At that moment Kathleen returned and said to her husband, "Our other guests will be here soon, Brian."

"We're just coming," he replied. He took his wife's arm, and led the way out of his study.

They assembled for lunch in the drawing room. As Aston was sitting quietly sipping his drink reflecting how events had moved so quickly, in walked Kathleen's guests. After a brief formal introduction Aston learned that the man was Archie Hovis, the vicar of Pellington. The gentle but frail looking lady was Miss

Jennifer Dowling, Kathleen's friend and French tutor to her son.

The cleric was short in stature and very portly. He dined well every evening, and enjoyed several glasses of the best claret. He came over as a bit pompous, but Aston didn't dislike the man, though he never stopped talking. On the whole he was a jovial chap, fond of eating and telling jokes.

Miss Dowling looked every bit of 80 years, but was aged 91. She was the first child of Miranda Dowling, a bond-servant who worked on a farm in the north of England, but who had escaped the tyranny of her cruel employer, and fled to France where she found employment in a dress shop.

Kathleen entered the room with her son. His eyes lit up when he saw Aston.

"Christopher, this is Mr Aston Wills."

"How do you do," he said politely, and they shook hands warmly.

After an interval everyone moved to the dining room for lunch. The meal was nourishing and the conversation light-hearted, that is, until it got round to religion. This shouldn't have surprised Aston, since he was surrounded by men of the cloth, and it is a topic of universal interest.

It was young Christopher who opened the discussion

by asking, "Parson, would you give us your idea of religion, and why it is that fewer people appear to attend church on Sundays?"

The cleric, not expecting this, gulped his wine and looked surprised. "I suppose it's because we have substituted a holiday for the holy day," he blurted out.

"What do you mean?" asked the young man.

Archie Hovis took a deep breath and said, "Well, our great-grandfathers called it the holy Sabbath; our grandfathers the sabbath; and our fathers called it Sunday. Today it's referred to as 'the weekend'."

There was a mixed look of approval and surprise on the faces of those seated around the table. The cleric helped himself to more wine.

Aston wanted to hear Brian's view on religion, so he asked, "Will you share some of your thoughts about this?"

Brian paused a moment before replying and said, "True religion comes from the heart, and should bring joy, love and peace into people's lives, not fear and guilt. Worship has meaning only when it's free. God is not honoured by subservient obedience to religious laws devoid of love and fellowship.

"I think it's important to realise that God's concern is for people, not religious structures. These exist merely to channel God's Word to His people. But it's people that

God is concerned about. He wants them to understand their lives and find happiness. Religion has become a burden to some people rather than something in which they find joy and comfort.

"The word religion has come to mean a list of rules and regulations, and this is the very thing God doesn't want. He created us to be free, to love Him and one another, in doing that to find happiness. It's all very simple really."

"I wonder if it is that simple," said the cleric. "It's not so simple to those sitting in the pews. They are like sheep and need to be told how to observe their religion. The old ideas have been tried and tested; how can they be thought to deprive people of their freedom?"

Brian looked sympathetically at Mr Hovis. "Most of what you say is true, but not quite the way you word it. In the past, religious leaders had the power to punish people for violating their religious observances. Many clergy believed that they had a mandate from God to control people's lives – even their thinking. So when people failed to obey, they were made to feel they were disobeying God. That cannot be right. God never intended that institutions should control people's lives."

There was silence for a few moments, then Kathleen asked, "Aston, what do you think of God?"

This question had troubled Aston for a long time. He

had not seriously discussed it with anyone, as far as he could remember. He was conscious that the assembled company were waiting.

Before he knew it words came tumbling out of his mouth. "Before all else God is good, and God is One. He is unique and cannot be compared to anyone or anything. I believe all creation expresses some facet of God's beauty. We need only look at the vast expanse of space beyond the stars to realise the unlimited comprehension of God's intelligence. Yet it seems to me there is much more to God than what is contained in the galaxy; though our careless use of nature's gifts and our abuse of the environment are damaging what God has so lovingly created."

Turning his attention to Kathleen, he said shyly, "Your mother once remarked that 'we can find God within ourselves, if we search deeply enough,' so I think that once we discover that God loves us, we have discovered the greatest joy in life."

"Thank you Wills, that was beautifully expressed," said Brian.

"Why don't you go out on the terrace," Kathleen suggested. "I'll join you presently."

Seated outside, with the sun shining overhead and bird songs sounding from the lush green trees surrounding the house, everyone felt what a restful place this home was.

"I really have to be going," Mr. Hovis said, as Kathleen reappeared.

"Do you have to?" she responded genuinely.

He left rather quickly, and as he disappeared he could be heard suppressing a belch!

Addressing Miss Dowling, Aston said, "Before you depart . . ." but she interrupted him. "I wasn't going just yet, until I've had a word with you."

"You want a word with me? That's strange," he said, "I was hoping to speak to you."

"Shall we sit over here," she suggested. Kathleen looked in their direction and smiled knowingly as she returned to the house flanked by the two men in her life.

"I understand you met Mary Whittacker many times," Jennifer said quietly, "and I hear that she welcomed you and encouraged you."

"Yes," Aston replied. "Did you know her?"

"I did. It was she who gave me shelter when I was homeless." Aston, trying not to look surprised, managed to say, "Homeless! But you look quite prosperous, if I may so."

"I am the most blessed of women, but I wasn't always as comfortable as I am now," she replied."Then one day I met Kathleen's mother; it was she who helped me find God and myself. From that day I was on the road to recovery."

"Mrs Whittacker was a remarkable woman," Aston confided. "But I can't remember ever hearing your name mentioned."

"Why should you? I was in Eastern Europe for many years, though we remained in touch by correspondence. But enough of me. What was it you wanted to ask me?"

Aston sensed this frail but saintly elderly lady was genuinely interested, and so he was able to respond openly without fear of ridicule.

"Why is it," he asked, "when God is a God of love, that there are so many children born to parents who fail to really love them, and even cause them harm?"

"The serene face of Jennifer Dowling was serious for a moment as if her thoughts were far away. It was some time before she answered.

"Whatever happens to us on earth does not alter the fact that God is a God of love, and in your heart you know that. When a man and woman have a child this places a sacred trust on them to see the child grow up, to give that life roots, and afterwards wings, in order that the young person may go forward and make a new life.

"The seeds of cruelty are inherent in the soul of each individual until God breathes new life into the spirit. He also sees purity of heart and sincerity of purpose. He knows that in spite of the weariness of the flesh, there is in every person the ability to rise above the early poverty of thought, the wrong teaching, the bad habits, and the mistakes made by us and to us in this school of life.

"In the beginning we are subject to what others do or may not do for us, but as we grow and gain knowledge, learn more of the truth and become stronger, we learn to detach ourselves from those things which do not give us peace, but rather leave us empty with no lasting satisfaction.

"What we live for determines what we see in life. We so often fail to see the things of the spirit because it isn't easy for people to think in spiritual terms. As the world of the senses is real, so is the world of the spirit, and people must be told about it even if it makes them feel uncomfortable."

She was silent for a while, then looking Aston directly in the eye, said very slowly, "When God's Spirit is awake in us it's then we understand the reality of the fact that we live. Try to realise for yourself the redeeming power of God's love; don't give up on your search for the living light of truth. Only then will the veil that separates you from heaven be lifted sufficiently for you to gain a greater understanding of why events in your life develop the way they do."

"That's strange," Aston said. "Mrs Whittacker was speaking on these lines just before she died."

"There's nothing strange about it, Mr Wills. The Spirit

of God chooses the people to convey His message to this world. He is here to make Jesus known, and open the eyes of unbelievers to the truth of the Word."

"What is the truth of the Word?" he asked.

There was compassion in her face mixed with some amusement as he asked his question. He suddenly realised the enormity of what he was asking, but he wanted to know her thoughts on the matter.

"I'll try and explain a little of what I know," she began, "but you will have to devote yourself to finding out more. A number of people will come into your life who will add to your knowledge, but your most important source will be the Spirit Himself. It's His direct action that will make the difference in your claims and presentation, and as you progress, I trust that you will give God the glory.

"In a little seed there is the possibility of growing food for sustenance or flowers and trees for beauty – all many times bigger than the seed itself. Every farmer knows he cannot reap a harvest until he plants the seed. It is the same with God's Word, it must be sown in the heart for it to come out of the mouth. If we don't know His Word, which reveals His will, how can we act on His word or know the truth about what He is saying?

"God's Word is truth and in His Word there is life. Jesus said, 'You shall know the truth and the truth shall set you free.' God does nothing without His Word; you have ample proof of that outlined in Genesis and elsewhere in Scripture, and also in creation itself.

"What is it that occupies the minds of most people?" she asked gently.

Aston tentatively put forward his theories on the most urgent of human needs. "To love and be loved is most desirable, with the added bonus of good health."

Miss Dowling agreed. "Our health is most important to us," she continued. "Nurses and medical practitioners in the community and in hospitals are God's chosen people to monitor and care for the nation's health. On the whole they do excellent work. But for a sick person to know that it is God's will they should be healed, the 'seed' must be planted in the mind and in the heart. Then it needs to be received and watered in faith and trust. Only then will it produce a harvest. Having knowledge of God's Word helps us to cooperate in our recovery."

As Aston listened to Jennifer Dowling speak so eloquently about the ways of the Spirit, he recalled Mary Whittacker quoting the scripture that said, "The prayer of faith will save the sick."

It began to dawn on him that if the farmer can have faith in the seed he sows, why can't the Christian have faith in the God of nature? Mary had tried to tell him this, but he had failed to understand.

At that moment Miss Dowling said, "One of the gifts of the Spirit is revelation. He is revealing to me that you will face grave opposition and even a brief stay in hospital which will test your faith and stamina. Be brave and trust in the Lord.

"Now I must be going. My car will be here soon. I am very punctual and I like things to be done decently and in order."

Aston hardly knew what to say, for at that moment he heard a car outside and the doorbell sounded. She simply waved her arm and said, "I leave you in His care." He never saw her again.

"Well, did you enjoy your cosy chat with Jenny? Kathleen asked.

"She was most helpful. Though I'd liked to have spent a little more time with her. I sensed she had more to say."

Kathleen smiled reassuringly. "Doesn't it say in the scriptures that God reveals His counsels in His own time, and doesn't tell us everything at once? Come and have some tea, then you will have to excuse me, I'll not be back before you leave, but I'm so pleased you came, and I trust you found your visit worthwhile!"

During tea Kathleen spoke proudly of Christopher's singing voice and how his rendering of 'Panis Angelicus' had won acclaim at the Welsh Eisteddfod. Kathleen prepared to leave and holding out her hand she wished Aston a safe journey home. Aston thanked Kathleen for her hospitality and she left.

"I'll be with you shortly," Brian said, as he accompanied his wife out of the room.

Aston sat alone with his thoughts, waiting for his host to return. The grandfather clock struck five chimes. As he listened to the sound he sat back on the soft cushions of the armchair and dreamily absorbed his surroundings. His thoughts wandered off into a meditation on time and eternity. He thought how few had yet grasped the reality that time is an illusion, that there is no past or future, only the present. The human mind can only experience the present in small measures; when the moment ends it is gone. Likewise, the future is a blank, it is void. Though it is present to God, it is outside the focus of human experience, unless revealed by God's Spirit.

Will the mind ever be able to understand that the past is still present and the future already is?

The sound of Brian's return broke his dreamy mood. "There is something I'd like to ask you," he said, as Brian entered the room.

"Go ahead," said Brian attentively.

"That Miss Dowling, she's one extraordinary lady. Is she real? I mean, she seemed to be in this world but not of it."

"You have answered your own question," said Brian

laughing. "She lives and walks in the spirit. Her whole life is devoted to the Lord. She was Mary's friend and now she is ours. Whatever she said to you out there, you can depend on it. She is only too aware that we are accountable to God for what we say, especially in matters to do with the soul."

Then, looking seriously for a moment, Brian said, "It isn't beyond the power of God to bestow upon those He chooses the ability to see and hear what others fail to understand, though it may be outside the scope of rational thinking.

"Now, you must be going," and placing his arm around Aston's shoulder, he walked him to the door. As he did so he gave him a gentle, reassuring smile and said, "Obedience to the Spirit will set you on the right path, Wills. But don't be surprised at the opposition and the attacks on your person. Keep faith and guard your health. Everything will come together as God has planned it. Go safely and go in peace."

He saw Aston to his car and waved goodbye.

The return journey towards London was slow and uncomfortable as the traffic built up. Aston reflected on all that had taken place during the past few hours. Brian had said, "There will be many distractions to lure you away from the path to which God is calling you; try not to be persuaded. There will be times when the prophetic word comes to you, and times when you wish it would, but God remains silent. You will have to learn to live with that silence.

"You will meet people who will mock God's glory and spit in your face when you defend it. But if you stand firm, your heart will rejoice over it as a gift from heaven."

Late one evening, as Aston was sitting in his study preparing his notes, he sensed a prompting in his spirit to pray for Jennifer Dowling, the quaint elderly lady with silvery white hair and contrasting young face, not beautiful with regard to her features, but beautiful because of her spiritual life. She would remain in Aston's memory as a selfless, humble servant of God, who believed in the abundance of His supply.

Her life was dedicated to making known the realities of the Spirit, but she who once "sought refuge in the shelter of the Most High, now rested in the shadows of the Almighty." In the silence of his heart he prayed for the repose of her soul.

Some months later Aston was admitted to hospital for surgery. It was complicated by a severe infection he picked up during his stay there. How could she have known?

His short acquaintance with this lady left him feeling

once again that God plants His saints where we least expect them.

All his engagements were cancelled and he began to lose confidence as his condition deteriorated. The treatment he received was not healing him. He recalled Jennifer's words: "Be brave and trust in the Lord." He decided it was time to go to The Healer.

He read in Isaiah about him "who forgives all our iniquities, and heals all our diseases." And he received comprehensive instructions from God's Word in Proverbs 4:20–22.

> My child, attend to my words; incline your ear to my sayings. Do not let them escape from your sight; keep them within your heart. For they are life to those who find them, and healing to all their flesh.

He meditated on these words and repeated them again and again. And he refused to be pulled down into depression any longer.

All heaven is behind God's Word. It is life to those who find it – not only to the flesh, but also to the soul. I cannot see the, soul, he reasoned, though I can observe expressions of it. The farmer cannot see the seed once it is planted. He believes it is growing before he sees it grow. This surely must be the "evidence of things not seen," and so it must be with the "seed" of the Word.

The only way a seed can do its work is by remaining in the soil; the only way God's "imperishable seed" can work in us is by keeping it near us, in our hearts. If God's Word has the power to heal us, then we must attend to it, search it out, and seek fellowship with Him. Aston began a sensible diet and encouraged himself in the Lord.

"The Lord is gracious and full of compassion; slow to anger and of great mercy. The Lord is good to all; His tender mercies are over all His works."

There was power in God's Word in the early church and Aston couldn't believe it had changed, or that it was not applicable to the present generation.

"Heaven and earth may pass away but my word will never pass away." God's Word does not change.

Brian's last words to him had been that "obedience to the Spirit will set you on the right path."

By God's grace he came to understand that the Holy Spirit is a living Person with a personality of His own, and was on the earth to be a Helper.

"Whoever believes in me, streams of living water will flow from him." The living water is the Spirit and whoever believes on His name and shows the things of Jesus to the world, the Spirit of God falls on him or her, as a gift from God.

As these thoughts encouraged him to maintain a positive attitude, Aston began to feel drawn towards the priesthood, but he dismissed the idea from his mind. After all, his diary was full and his life was mapped out. Besides, he wasn't sure that he had the stomach for all that obedience, and what he had seen of some clergy didn't inspire him.

Then he remembered Mary saying that the early apostles were not shining examples of obedience. They argued for management positions, deserted the Boss when the going got tough, and one openly denied any knowledge of Him. But this hadn't stopped them from responding to the call of the Holy Spirit. He breathed fire into their souls and they went out and declared the works of the Lord.

One of them, Peter, addressed the crowds at Pentecost. The Bible says the people were "cut to the heart, and cried out 'what shall we do?'"

It was some two years later. Aston's health had began to recover and soon he was fully restored. As part of his restoration regime, he would recite God's Word over and over to himself as he walked by the river close to Barchester Cathedral, a place he often liked to visit.

One day, he saw some children playing on the grass, with their parents close by. Aston had a great love of these little ones and stopped to talk to them within hearing of the adults. He laughed with them at the children's playful games and the trivial things they said that were important to them.

"You are God's children," he said to them, "and He loves you just as your parents do." He told them that they should enjoy their childhood and not grow up before their time.

As he continued his walk he met Brian's father and Mary's friend, the Rev'd Canon James Brookes.

James was seated under a willow tree and he beckoned Aston over to join him.

"Hello, sir," Aston said. "This is a pleasant surprise. But you're not here by chance ?

"You are very astute, Wills, and quite right. The correct decision has been made," he said, half smiling to himself.

"What decision is that?" Aston asked.

"We would like you to offer yourself for ordination, if you feel called to it," the canon answered.

Aston was not usually lost for words, but at this suggestion he just sat there. After a few moments he said, "It has been on my mind, but for some reason I was hesitant. I mean, it's a big step and I have to be sure that God is calling me to serve Him in this way."

"Then you'll give it serious thought and pray about it?" the canon asked.

"I will," Aston replied.

Then the two men chatted about Mary and Gordon, and Gordon's garden. "I was never gifted with green fingers," Aston said, "but I do have a few pots scattered around the place."

Aston was encouraged by Canon Brookes, who became the spiritual father he had so longed for throughout his life. They met as often as they could and Aston learned more of the Christian life as revealed in scripture and ordained by God. During the next few weeks he began the long process of being considered for ordination to the priesthood.

Canon Brookes proved to be a faithful friend and mentor. He encouraged Aston in all aspects of the priestly life, but he had to face the rigorous selection committee alone. It was not easy. Some of the bishop's advisors were men of steel, though others were gentle, compassionate and understanding.

Eventually, Aston came before his final selector. The archdeacon came to his home and, after speaking for several minutes, announced that he would not be recommending Aston to the bishop. His actual words to Aston were, "You are not top drawer."

Aston was devastated, his hopes dashed by the contemptuous remarks made by someone supposedly representing the church of God on earth. The words hit deep into his spirit and for the next few years he sought consolation in various schools of philosophy.

It was much later that Aston met his former mentor. He was attending a lecture on ageing given by Dr Ramanhansa from the World Health Organisation. Sharing the platform with him was the Rev'd James Brookes.

At the conclusion of the meeting Aston waited to speak to the Canon. He was delighted to see him and asked how he was. Aston told him about his adventures into other religions and philosophical paths.

"Have you got it out of your system now?" he asked. Aston nodded. "Well now perhaps you will do what God is calling you to do," he said sternly.

"But what about . . ." Aston began. James Brookes didn't let him finish. "Dismiss those people from your mind. God has moved them on to new pastures. You will not experience the same difficulties again."

Aston went through the entire process again, this time with different assessors, and was eventually admitted to Barchester Theological College to begin training for the priesthood.

Three years later he walked in procession with 20 other ordinands up the aisle of the famous cathedral towards a new life. As the procession entered the church it was an impressive sight with the supporting clergy, acolytes, chaplains, the archdeacon and the bishop following behind.

Aston, with his hands folded and palms pressed together, looked straight ahead as if absorbed in thoughts about things far away. The procession made its way up the aisle towards the sanctuary.

The ordinands took their place. Aston glanced round quickly as the bishop made his way into the sanctuary. He saw Brian and Kathleen sitting just a few rows back. They exchanged smiles and Aston was grateful for the presence of his faithful friends.

Standing next to the bishop and the new archdeacon was Canon James Brookes. He looked impressive in his priestly robes, tall and scholarly looking. His silvery hair was slightly wavy, and his metal-rimmed glasses increased his intellectual appearance.

The entrance hymn came to an end and the bishop greeted the people. The Gloria was sung and the liturgy of the Word continued. After the Gospel the bishop gave a moving address. The ordinands were presented by the archdeacon, and the bishop asked the congregation to uphold them in their ministry.

In his declaration the bishop said, "Priests are called to proclaim the word of the Lord, to call their hearers to repentance . . . to baptise . . . to preside at the celebration of the Holy Communion . . . to lead people in prayer and worship . . . to teach and encourage them by word and example . . . to minister to the sick . . ."

"You are to be messengers, watchmen, and stewards of the Lord . . . search for God's children in the wilderness of this world's temptations . . . guide them through its confusions . . .

"Because you cannot bear the weight of this ministry in your own strength but only by the grace and power of God, pray earnestly for His Holy Spirit . . . so that you may grow stronger and more mature in your ministry."

The declarations made by each ordinand were powerful and binding. At the moment of ordination the bishop placed his hands on the head of each candidate. When he came to Aston, James Brookes stepped forward and extended his right hand towards his protégé as the bishop said, "Send down the Holy Spirit upon your servant, Aston, for the office and work of a priest in your church."

Brian was watching from his pew as the bishop called on God to bless his servant with the gift of the Holy Spirit, and in the silence of his heart he prayed, "May God have mercy on your soul as you accept this awesome responsibility."

After the stoles had been turned round the service continued with the Peace and the Eucharist. During the administration Christopher's voice could be heard from the choir stalls singing "Panis Angelicus". Aston paused for a moment as he was administering the chalice, and a gentle smile appeared on his face as he made his way along the line of parishioners kneeling at the altar rail.

The liturgy, though stripped of much of the medieval pageantry that once characterised these ceremonies, was still very impressive. The rich traditions of the church were mystically reflected in this beautiful and timeless rite.

The ceremony over, the ordinands met with their families and friends, some to go on and celebrate over a meal, others to spend the night in prayer.

What started out as one man's desire to help a family in need ended with his own life being enriched in the greatest possible way. He went on to serve the Lord, and though he made his mistakes and errors, was hurt by the injustices of the men who were his colleagues in ministry, torn apart in his personal life by misfortune, yet he overcame these human tragedies and consecrated his life to God. I'm pleased to say there is much documented evidence which attest to his thorough and loving ministry.

Canon James Brookes finally retired to a small country church to be near his son, and Brian was made suffragan bishop in the county he loved to call his home, with Kathleen at his side loving and supporting him.

Aston Wills was sent to a parish in the city to serve out his second curacy. The neighbourhood was run down and neglected, graffiti was scrawled on many buildings, there was high unemployment and little recreation. Most of the people had hearts of gold but others had yet to be reached with the message that caring and loving are the sunbeams and raindrops that nurture the personality into maturity.

Aston wrote many lengthy articles for the local newspapers speaking against racial prejudice and the social injustices that plagued the community. Not everyone agreed with his liberal views and some responded in strong rhetoric, but he continued to defend his position and also worked hard encouraging others to make greater provision for the elderly. He was delighted with the response from the local services and volunteers and worked alongside them to ensure its continued success.

Some months before he was due to move to another appointment as priest in charge of a large parish, he became the victim of much abuse and there were threats on his life.

One Sunday evening, as Aston was relaxing at his home, he heard a knock at the front door. Answering it he saw a gaunt and poorly dressed young man standing on the doorstep. Aston removed the security chain from the door and, as he opened it, two other men appeared from out of the darkness. All three pounced on him, knocking him to the floor. In the struggle Aston was stabbed several times. His last words as he lay dying were, "I forgive you, may God have mercy on my soul."

His dying words were heard by one of the three assailants, who afterwards confessed to the police. All three were imprisoned, though the one with a conscience was given a lighter sentence and later gave his life to Christ.

The whole community was outraged at this senseless act of violence for the killers took only money and clothing from the house.

Aston's death brought the people together. Part of his last sermon was reproduced in the local newspapers and the parish magazine:

Love Has a Message

The greatest love story in the entire world is God's love for us. His love is a gospel to be lived out, to bring us into harmonious relationships. Yet certain people continue to live under the dark clouds of prejudice that divided families and communities. The god of this world has deceived their minds, so they behave in a cruel and irrational manner.

Many hearts are broken through separation, lives torn apart by lack of love, foolish mistakes and thoughtlessness.

If, in the language of romance, there is no greater and deeper wound than the arrow of love, how much more bitter and painful is the sword of hatred that pierces the heart? Its sting has lasting consequences and remains one of the great human tragedies of our time. Bitter words are not what cause pain, though they may be unpleasant, it's that the one who loves you should have said them.

Mistakes are made in nearly every relationship. It's only genuine love that makes it possible to accept the limitations of another person. Offering one's partner love that has a healing quality helps that person to accept himself or herself as a whole person.

To love another is to desire what is good for them, and so enrich their life. Just as a flower opens its petals to the light, so does the human heart respond to the warm embrace of genuine love. That's why I often encourage you to give each other a "holy hug."

A kind smiling face can be used by God to radiate the sunshine of healing, to a cold embittered heart and lonely soul.

It's time to put a stop to hatred and prejudice and to use our skills and energies to heal the wounds of our community, to build an environment that is safe for all our children and a place where the elderly can grow old in peace.

No matter how we define love, we can't get away from the fact that love is the ability to establish healthy, meaningful relationships with other human beings, understanding that they too are struggling with the pressures of life. Knowing that we are loved for ourselves, that someone

> cares, our lives begin to unfold more successfully and we learn to understand who we are, so that when pain and disappointments visit our door we shall have the strength to deal effectively and wisely with them.

The tributes that came pouring in, expressing affection for the man and his ministry, caused many people to realise how little they had known him. The newspaper editors ended their report in much the same way. "His was a good life ended prematurely."

You will find people like Mary, Brian, Wills and the Canon living in every community. They are the ones who believe in you, want the best for you, and wish you to know that you are valued and precious as a human being.